# SIX MYTHS ABOUT THE GOOD LIFE

## Thinking about What Has Value

Joel J. Kupperman

# SIX MYTHS ABOUT THE GOOD LIFE

*Thinking about What Has Value*

Hackett Publishing Company, Inc.
Indianapolis/Cambridge

For further information, please address

Hackett Publishing Company, Inc.
P.O. Box 44937
Indianapolis, IN 46244-0937

www.hackettpublishing.com

Cover design by Abigail Coyle
Text design by Elizabeth Wilson
Composition by Brighid Willson
Printed at Edwards Brothers, Inc.


**Library of Congress Cataloging-in-Publication Data**

Kupperman, Joel.
  Six myths about the good life: thinking about what has value / Joel J. Kupperman.
     p. cm.
  Includes bibliographical references.
  ISBN 0-87220-783-8 (cloth : alk. paper) — ISBN 0-87220-782-X (pbk. : alk. paper)
  1. Happiness. 2. Success. 3. Quality of life. 4. Conduct of life. I. Title.
  BJ1481.K87 2006
  17—dc22
                                                2005020868

The paper used in this publication meets the minimum requirements of
American National Standard for Information Sciences—Permanence of Paper
for Printed Library Materials, ANSI Z39.48–1984.

# Contents

# Preface

This book represents an attempt to write good philosophy for a readership that would consist largely of intelligent nonspecialists, including people with very little prior knowledge of philosophy. It seemed to me that it could be done: John Perry, Peter Singer, and (closer to the territory of this book) John Kekes provided some successful recent models. But clearly it was not going to be easy.

Writing style was always a concern; I was helped by a copyeditor friend, Julie Tamarkin, whose first-stage copyediting undoubtedly made the manuscript more tolerable to its first readers. There are a number of people to whom I am grateful for helpful suggestions or pointers or timely encouragement, or some combination of these. Let me express thanks to Pam Benson, Norman Fiering, John Kekes, Donald Kelley, Karen Ordahl Kupperman, Peter Ohlin, Bonnie Smith, David Wong, and especially my editor at Hackett, Deborah Wilkes. Three anonymous readers for Hackett made unusually helpful suggestions.

Let me express gratitude to the Positive Psychology Network, led by Martin Seligman, for inviting me to their conferences at Akumal in 2001. This led to a discussion group in New York that included at various times Paul Rozin, Claude Fischler, Daniel Kahneman, and Alan Page Fiske. I am especially grateful to Paul Rozin and Alan Fiske for their comments on a paper, "Comfort, Hedonic Treadmills, and Public Policy," which was the precursor of the first chapter of this book.

Thanks also to the University of Connecticut Humanities Institute, directed by Richard D. Brown with Francoise Dussart, for a fellowship in 2003–4 that propelled this book (and a simultaneous project, *Ethics and Qualities of Life*) forward, and to the National Endowment for the Humanities for a fellowship in 2004–5 that allowed me to finish both books in a timely manner. In the final two weeks of the revision process, I benefited from the hospitality of the National Humanities Center.

Chapter 1 of this book has some overlap with "Comfort, Hedonic Treadmills, and Public Policy," *Public Affairs Quarterly* 17 (2003); the final chapter has some overlap with "The Epistemology of Noninstrumental Value," *Philosophy and Phenomenological Research* 65 (2005). I am grateful to both journals for permission to include this overlapping material.

# Introduction

This book is about good lives—lives that are both desirable and enviable—and about what is important to them. There is a problem of method, though. The topic of good lives is to a large extent resistant to generalizations. What is important and wonderful in one good life may be deleterious in another. Imagine a book about "Great Paintings" or "Great Poems." What kinds of general truths could it legitimately convey?

There are important truths, though, that deny easy and attractive generalizations. These generalizations come as thoughts about good lives, in many cases ideas that were handed down to us. Often they have a nugget of truth, which is then exaggerated or oversimplified. They may fit one kind of good life better than other kinds. Often they simply represent what we would like to believe.

One assumption underlying this book is that everyone could benefit from thinking further, and in less simplistic ways, about good lives. Another is that a useful first step is to summon up obvious and appealing generalizations and to see what is faulty about them. Prominent in the work of some philosophers (in the twentieth century notably Ludwig Wittgenstein) is the idea that thinking effectively about life requires philosophical therapy, loosening the hold of attractive and simple ideas that get in the way of our intelligence.

"Philosophical therapy" can be appreciated in relation to a central characteristic of philosophy, at least in the West since the time of Socrates and Plato. This lies in the importance of argument, of being able to argue for one's conclusions. In much philosophical writing, the relation of argument to conclusions is clearly marked; often the conclusion then is presented with an air of "Here is the truth; all inquiry into these topics now may cease." There is something faintly comical in this, especially because inquiry into the topics usually does not cease.

An idea that underlies much of Wittgenstein's therapy suggests that most of us gravitate to generalizations which cover a range of cases, some of which are significantly different from others. The generalizations are appealing because most of us would like not to think too much, or to pay close attention to the variations among particular cases. Wittgenstein's attitude comes out in an anecdote by Norman Malcolm, an American who had gone to Cambridge University to study with Wittgenstein. Malcolm had remarked that a German claim (in the fall of 1939) that the British government had instigated an assassination attempt against Hitler could not possibly be true. It went against his sense of British national character. This made Wittgenstein very angry. He considered it "a great stupidity and also an indication that I was not learning anything from the philosophical training he was trying to give me."[1] Presumably Wittgenstein saw it as a vast oversimplification to think that knowledge of an individual's or a nation's character allows one to predict with certainty how the individual or nation will behave over time in a variety of situations.[2]

In the "philosophical therapy" approach, arguments will consist largely of considerations that undermine attractive but superficial views. A large part of the conclusion, then, is that one needs to think further. In the end, you have to find your own way out.

This book is an attempt to pursue this approach in relation to issues about what is a good life. No specific formulas for what is a good life will be presented. Considerations that often matter will be pointed to, and both the appeal and the flaws of easy generalizations will be examined. None of the Six Myths is a total mistake, but neither is any of them entirely right. In the end, the reader who accepts the arguments in this book will have to do her or his own thinking about what can constitute a good life.

A book that aims to facilitate this needs to be as direct and untechnical as possible. Each of the chapters is designed to be as uncluttered as possible. References and elaborating remarks are kept to a minimum. Some of the text (especially in the opening chapter) inevitably will presuppose a view of larger philosophical issues, or will touch on related issues of importance. Any interested reader deserves disclosure of this, but such explanations could clutter the text unbearably. They accordingly are merely noted in the text, and have been gathered in the Appendix.

1. Norman Malcolm, *Ludwig Wittgenstein. A Memoir* (London: Oxford University Press, 1958), 32–33.

2. For one view of what character is, see my *Character* (New York: Oxford University Press, 1991).

# *Myth One*

## PURSUING COMFORT AND PLEASURE WILL LEAD TO THE BEST POSSIBLE LIFE

Most of us in our unreflective moods think of the good life—the one that would feel like a reward—as being extremely comfortable and pleasant. Not everyone who we think deserves such a life gets it. Some do good for others and achieve important goals, while scoring low in comfort or pleasure. This is bad luck, and we feel sorry for them. What we all seem to want is more comfort and more pleasure.

That is a simple view, and may represent a tendency that is wired into normal human nature. Can the judgment that the best life is one of great comfort and great pleasure survive reflection? In order to sort this out, we need to think more about what are comfort and pleasure, and about the varieties of comforts and pleasures. Then we can ask to what the pursuit of increased comfort and pleasure leads, and also whether it is a general truth that a very pleasant and comfortable life is the most rewarding.

## A First Look at Pleasure and Its Values

The word "value" here stands in for how rewarding or unrewarding something is. One way of getting at the nature of pleasure (and then at its value) is to contrast it with happiness. Some people (including some philosophers and psychologists) think of "pleasure" and "happiness" as virtually interchangeable words, but they refer to different kinds of things.

Pleasures typically last a fairly short time, whereas there is a sense in which someone can be happy for a summer, a year, or a lifetime. Pleasures

1

also have an object; that is, you are pleased by such and such—some particular thing or experience—and this often is the cause of the pleasure and in what you take pleasure. Happiness, in the sense in which you can be happy for years, is about nothing in particular; you will be happy about life in general. It would sound odd to say that you are pleased, but not by anything in particular. That would not be pleasure. It would be a good mood.

Our pleasure in something is an agreeable feeling, and typically someone who is experiencing pleasure is aware of a positive affect. Is pleasure merely an agreeable feeling? There is reason to think that there is more to pleasure than that. It sounds odd to say, "It was pleasant, but I would never want to experience that again." This combination at the least would require explanation. It looks like pleasure is not only an agreeable feeling, but also typically must have a role in our desires for the future.

Pleasure and wanting to have more normally go together. Occasionally one occurs without the other, and initially this seems hard to understand. There can be, however, explanations of what otherwise would seem hardly intelligible. Perhaps there is some moral or prudential reason not to want the pleasure repeated?

Indeed, one of the criteria for thinking that something was pleasant for a person (if there is any doubt) is that, all things being equal, that person would like more of it. Typically what satisfies the most obvious criterion for pleasure—that someone feels good in an activity or about something—will also satisfy the requirement that, other things being equal, that person would like more of the same.

If something satisfies one of the criteria and not the other one, we may find it difficult to know what to say. Wanting more of what did not feel good can seem more a matter of a compulsive need than of pleasure. But in some cases we may wonder whether it really did not feel good. Masochists, for example, may enjoy certain kinds of moderate pain.

Enjoying the feeling but (even with other things being equal) wanting never again to experience whatever gave it, or what it was about, presents an even more problematic combination. However, this combination can be made plausible. Perhaps the pleasure was not all that great, and you simply prefer variety in your pleasurable experiences?

The word "happy" sometimes does parallel "pleased" in taking a specific object. You can be happy about something, though being happy in this sense often lasts only a short time. However there is a global sense of happiness in which someone can be happy, period. As already noted, this is a basic feeling about life that can last for a long time. When people say that they want happiness, they are talking about this global sense.

A neat-minded person might say that this (global) happiness is the sum of pleasures minus pains. But lived experience is not neat. As we will see in the next chapter, someone can have many pleasures but a basic feeling about life that is not positive, and not be happy. There are cases also when someone is happy with not very many pleasures.

Given this, many reflective people come to think that the good life can be equated with one of happiness. The next chapter will show that this too is a mistake. Happiness, nevertheless, often is very important in a good life. Are pleasures important? This has been a subject of philosophical worry for more than two thousand years.

Plato, in his dialogue *Philebus,* argues that the correct answer to "How valuable are pleasures?" is "It depends." This is more complicated than the most common view. Pleasure generally is nice. Because of this, a response to Plato's question that many people find immediately plausible is that pleasure is always worth having. It is then tempting to say that the most rewarding life will be the one with the most pleasure (minus pain). This view is known as hedonism.[1] Maybe there is an element of hedonism in almost everyone, in that almost everyone has moments in which what seems most important is to have more pleasure or to avoid pain. Most of us can feel the appeal of hedonism. But it is far too simple a view, and Plato was one of the first to argue against it.

If pleasure really determines how rewarding one's life is, then one should consider any life that is filled with pleasure (and without pain) as enviable. Plato asks whether you would be willing to trade your life for that of a clam that is in a continuous state of great pleasure. (Imagine that that grain of sand is in just the right place, so that the clam's whole life is

---

1. Hedonism is especially associated with the views of two famous thinkers: the ancient Greek philosopher Epicurus and the nineteenth-century English philosopher John Stuart Mill. However, Epicurus placed much more emphasis on avoiding suffering than on gaining and augmenting pleasure. A similar emphasis on avoiding suffering emerges in Mill's account in Chapter 2 of *Utilitarianism* of what a happy life would be like. This accords with what psychologists have called "negativity bias": our tendency to regret losses more than we value gains. See Paul Rozin and Ed Royzman, "Negativity Bias, Negativity Dominance, and Contagion," *Personality and Social Psychology Review* 5 (1999), 296–320.

a crescendo of pleasure.) If something is holding you back from the idea of trading lives, then perhaps there are other things besides pleasure that are important? Also, maybe some pleasures—however nice they may feel—do not really amount to much?

A natural thought also is this. If pleasure is generally pleasure *in* something particular, then the value of the pleasure might depend on in what pleasure was taken. Alice feels pleasure in making an important scientific discovery, and Mabel feels an equal degree of pleasure in completing her collection of bottle caps; are the two pleasures of equal value? What of the keen pleasure experienced by a sadist after a good day at the torture chamber? That the sadist can feel great pleasure is undeniable. That the pleasure—because, taken by itself it is an occurrence of pleasure—has great value can be debated.

This presents an issue important to ethical philosophy, and to life. Is the standard for the value of an experience or in a life simply how much the person (whose experience or life it is) likes it? Or can we legitimately second-guess that person, and say, "He (or she) thinks it is wonderful, but really it is not"?

These are thorny questions. The view that people can be wrong about what they think are values in their lives might seem antidemocratic and elitist.[2] On the other hand—as we will see in the next chapter—there are cases in which someone is happy with a life that no one would envy. Would you trade lives with an idiot, if the idiot's pleasures were greater?

## Pleasures and Subjective Well-Being

Even apart from the issue of whether quality of life can be judged, as it were, from the outside, there are reasons for thinking that not all pleasures are alike in value. These are found in the psychological research on subjective well-being. Subjective well-being means how people estimate their own satisfactions. One well-known study is Mihaly Csikszentmihalyi's

---

2. There are other reasons why many are suspicious of the view that people can be wrong about what they think are values in their lives. These are taken up and discussed in the Appendix, Number 1.

*Flow: The Psychology of Optimal Experience.* Csikszentmihalyi's data show that people most value experiences in which they have carried on a sequence of skilled activities and have been caught up in them, as the book's title suggests.[3] The activities could be musical, athletic, artistic, intellectual, involve furniture-making, etc.

These are active pleasures, generally requiring alertness; and they have some interesting connections with a person's sense of self. Genuine skills need to be acquired, a process that often involves effort, so that they represent achievements. There then has to be a background element of pride in being absorbed in skilled activity. The pride contributes to self-esteem. There is a long tradition in Western culture of being suspicious of pride, but this surely refers to excessive pride. Someone who has nothing to be proud of is in real trouble. One way of gaining pride is to attempt difficult things, which might involve acquiring skills, and to succeed.

You can lose yourself in skilled activity. One of the paradoxes of the classic literature of self-fulfillment, both Asian and Western, is that this kind of loss of self can also represent something extremely positive about one's self: something that is all the more powerful for not being the primary object of attention. Loss of self can be an ego trip. This is one reason why it is claimed that many saints and mystics experience joy.

Even apart from that, some philosophers (for example, the nineteenth-century German philosopher Arthur Schopenhauer) have pointed out ways in which self-concern can be like an uncomfortable background noise in experience. At the least it is a mild irritant. The irritant disappears when you lose yourself in an activity or a line of thought; Schopenhauer was particularly struck by the loss of self-concern in aesthetic experience. Being taken out of oneself in this way is gratifying. All of these ideas come together in books like the ancient Indian *Bhagavad Gita,* which centers on the claim that loss of self in activity is both liberating and a source of joy. To borrow current sports slang: the best life, the *Gita* suggests, is spent as much as possible in "the zone."

Csikszentmihalyi contrasts the highly rated satisfactions of sequenced skillful activity with some common passive pleasures, such as watching television. His data show that over an extended period this passive pleasure cumulatively is a mild depressive. At best, the pleasure of this kind of

3. There is a possible objection at this point, which is plausible but I think not convincing. It will be discussed in the Appendix, Number 2.

activity is only slightly good, whereas people report the pleasure of sequenced skillful activity as very good. This provides contemporary psychological evidence to support Plato's view of the value of pleasures: namely, that it depends on the type of pleasure.[4]

Csikszentmihalyi's data also give reason to reject another of the attractively over-simple views that have found their way into philosophy: that what we want (or, in some loose sense, desire) is how we know what is valuable for us. People who watch a lot of television must want to do it. The passivity of watching, with its minimal demandingness, represents a seductive relaxation and extreme initial mental comfort. The fact that it is mildly pleasant but over a period of time cumulatively depressive suggests that there can be a large class of cases in which what we desire is not in our best interests. Other examples can be found among alcoholics and drug addicts.

Ethical philosophers sometimes have been tempted by the thought that there must be a sense of value, something that tells us what is desirable in life much as our five senses tell us what is real in the world. John Stuart Mill nominated desire as the sense of value. His argument for pleasure as the fundamental good was that pleasure is involved when we desire anything.[5]

In fact, there is no perfect candidate to be the sense of value; just as our senses sometimes deceive us, any indicator of value that we might rely on could be highly misleading. But desire looks like an especially weak candidate. The motivational tug that typically is an element of emotions is especially prominent in desire, and can conflict with a person's reflective evaluative judgment of what is desired.[6] Also, desire is an emotion that looks forward in time; we often think that we are in a better position to evaluate something when we are experiencing it than when we are merely looking forward to it. For these reasons there might be better can-

---

4. The suggestion here in effect takes sides in a long-running philosophical debate about the relation between the "is" (in this instance, psychological data) and the "ought," or facts and values. This will be discussed, with some justification of the position that this chapter presupposes, in the Appendix, Number 3.

5. A case for holding that Mill was right in finding a deep connection between desire and pleasure will be developed in the Appendix, Number 4.

6. The nature of emotions is relevant to much of this book. One theme that will emerge is that good lives typically require emotional adjustments. Another is that awareness of what is good or not so good typically takes shape in emotional states. Think of what delight, admiration, boredom, disgust, and contempt sometimes tell us. A view of what emotions are will be presented in the Appendix, Number 5.

didates to count as senses of value. An especially plausible (but hardly perfect) candidate is delight.

## Pleasure, Pain, and Hedonic Treadmills

There is a separate reason to think that the key to a good life is not the quantity of pleasure minus pain. Human psychology may entail built-in constraints on how favorable the balance (of pleasures minus pains) can be, and hence drastic improvement in quality of life must take another form. There are two arguments that point in this direction. One is found in the teachings of Buddha (c. 500 BCE), a philosopher who founded a movement to transform people's lives that has taken on many different forms over the centuries. The other is found in recent psychological literature.

Pleasure, Buddha contends, presupposes desire. You want something, and then you get it or keep it, which gives pleasure. However, the role of desire in his view carries some persistent disadvantages. First, the state of desiring something and not having it is not pleasant. Normally it is frustrating. But this frustration is intimately connected with the pleasure. Indeed it could be argued that the pleasure depends on frustration.

Consider these two examples. First, imagine whatever it is that you think would be the keenest possible pleasure. Imagine a world in which, whenever you wanted something, you would have it within two seconds. It is easy to see that in this world of extreme instant gratification, whatever might have been exciting and memorable would become boring and humdrum.

Secondly, even a humble pleasure could become intense given the right level of frustration. Take that of drinking a simple glass of water. You could turn this into something really intense. Simply don't have anything to drink for the next few days, and then have a glass of water.

If it is agreed that pleasure requires and depends on frustration, then what had looked positive (pleasures) now looks like part of a zero-sum game. But it may be worse than that. Pleasure makes up for the antecedent frustration. But sometimes we want something very much (with all of the frustration) and then don't get it. This happens to people especially when they are sick, or old, or dying. In light of this, the zero-sum game begins to look as if it is headed toward a negative. Desire entails suffering, and the sources of suffering can multiply.[7]

In classic Buddhist texts this argument is given a disturbing twist. The problem of desire is not merely its link with frustration and suffering. The suggestion also is that desire (much like some drugs) is addictive. In the abstract, you might think that you desire such-and-such, and that when you get it the process will be finished. But no—the Buddhist philosopher suggests—by now you are hooked on desire, and even if you have got what you wanted, you will go on to want something more. You will become a desire junkie. This will lead to a life of suffering. It is extremely difficult to kick the habit of desiring "cold turkey"; one reason why Buddhism developed into a movement was to provide institutional structures that would make it more possible.

One feature of the desire and suffering problem deserves comment. Part of the story is that desiring (and then suffering) is part of normal human nature, which we all start out with. Most of us think of what is natural to all or almost all of us human beings as having a special claim to consideration, in relation to many practical questions. We sometimes say "That's human nature," as if this settles any question.

At the least, what is natural will be taken as a default position. But it can be argued that what is natural represents an evolutionary process, and that the results of this process might have worked well at the early stages or in primitive states of civilization—and maybe not so well now. The Australian philosopher J. J. C. Smart once, half-jokingly, nominated the sinus as evidence of evolution. As he pointed out, its drainage functions would have worked quite well originally if one posits human forebearers who moved on all fours. But now we walk upright, and the sinus is no longer an ideal device. Perhaps the desire-pleasure nexus is no longer entirely ideal?

---

7. It is instructive that the Buddhist warning against desire is put in terms of its vulnerability to what is translated as suffering, rather than to pain. The promise is that the disciplined Buddhist adept can have a life without suffering. It would be impossible to promise a life without pain because, for one thing, virtually everyone has pain nerves in the body. If something impacts on these nerves in the right way, pain will result. Suffering, on the other hand, is largely a matter of how pain is processed. Buddha's view was that someone who is disciplined and has control over her or his mind would not experience suffering even if there is pain. Pain and suffering will be discussed in the Appendix, Number 6.

Much of classical Indian philosophy, both Buddhist and that associated with Hinduism, claims that for us, as we are now, normal human nature is a trap. We are born with intense desires, crying about what we want to avoid and grabbing what we want. No doubt these personality settings have their uses, but they can become damaging at the point at which we are mature, reflective, and autonomous. They lead to pleasure seeking, suffering, and a loss of focus on what really matters. Their inadequacy is manifested in a scarcity of joy in most of our lives.

The Indian texts, in various ways, urge us to give up pleasures and to adapt ourselves for a life of joy. The kind of joy they have in mind is objectless, and distinct from pleasure in a number of ways. Unlike pleasure, it is not *in* something; it is a global exhilaration. Unlike pleasure also, it does not have predictable occasions.[8] Despite this, its likelihood can be increased hugely, it is claimed, by an emptying out of concerns and distractions, and the practice of a quiet contemplation.

All of this adds up to one argument that pleasure cannot be an important element in a really good life. It costs too much. And anyway, it is less thoroughly satisfactory than joy. If we want to improve our lives drastically, then it might be smarter to go for joy than for a much better balance of pleasure over pain (which the argument suggests is in the long run unattainable).

---

8. Translations normally are not exact, and word choice can vary among translators. "Joy" is a favored term in translations of Indian philosophy for what an enlightened person can expect to experience. In some translations of Buddhist texts the word "bliss" is chosen.

"Joy" and "bliss" are not synonyms, although both words, like words for emotional states in general, cover a range of cases, and cases of what might be called "joy" can overlap with ones of what could be termed "bliss." Generally, "joy" is more likely to be used for an exhilarating rush of positive affect that is about nothing in particular. The poet Wordsworth's "surprised by joy" is a good example, and there is a long tradition of people whose joy is connected with immersion in nature. "Bliss" is more likely to be used when the positive affect is steady state and oceanic. Neither joy nor bliss is as generally well understood as pleasure, in part because so many pleasures are either biologically based or embedded in the circumstances of ordinary life. Joy and bliss in contrast are often said to be made possible by a kind of spiritual cleansing, or emptying out of concerns and prejudgments. This is nicely put by the poem in the Chinese Daoist Daodejing that says (in the Blakney translation) that "The way (the Daoist path that will yield joy) is gained by daily loss." Whatever the reason, it seems widely agreed that busy, efficient people (however satisfactory their lives will be in many respects) are unlikely to experience much joy.

It is worth pointing out that there is at least one loophole in this argument. Even if we accept the Buddhist view of desires—that they are addictive, and introduce something into life that verges on mental illness—the firmness of the link between pleasure and desire can be questioned. Perhaps some pleasures do not require or generate desires?

The largest class of exceptions would consist of what might be termed pleasures of spontaneity. These pleasures typically are not sought in any way that involves a sense of hunger or need. They simply happen, in a way that may not be the result of directed activity. And then, after they happen, we simply move on.

Here are two simple examples. You are talking with friends, and suddenly someone hands you a bit of food that turns out to be perfectly delicious. It is pleasant, even though there was no frustration or arousal before the experience. When you have eaten it, you resume your conversation. A second example is what happens when you encounter friends, whose conversation you enjoy, on the street, or when you suddenly hear some music that you really like. Again, frustration or arousal, or post-pleasure longing, need not be part of this picture.

To be clear: it may be that nothing in the last two paragraphs is an argument against the actual views of Buddha or of other Indian philosophers who decried what is translated as "pleasure." The translations from Pali or Sanskrit can be inexact. It may be that what is translated as "pleasure" in fact refers to a subset of what we think of as pleasures, namely those that involve longing and attachment.

The word "desire" also deserves comment. In recent years it has been used loosely, especially by certain philosophers, to refer to any preference that motivates us. The traditional meaning of "desire" was limited to rather strongly felt preferences, in which the element of psychological attachment (to what was desired) was such that losing or not getting it would be strongly felt.

Desire, in this stronger and more specific sense, is somewhat akin to craving. Certainly your mild preferences would not count as desires. If someone gives you a choice between vanilla and chocolate ice cream, and you say, "If it's all the same to you, I guess I'll take chocolate" (while not really minding if you then are given vanilla), this preference for chocolate does not qualify as desire given the traditional meaning.

This traditional meaning of desire makes intelligible the tight connection that Buddha assumes between desire and suffering. "Desire" in the broad and looser sense of preference that motivates you, on the other hand, makes no sense as a translation of what Buddha urges us to lose and claimed to have lost himself. He clearly preferred to teach his message of liberation rather than lead a private life. Further, it would be impossible for anyone to function even in the most low-key way if she or he had no preferences whatsoever.

The second argument that suggests caution regarding a more favorable balance of pleasures over pains as the key to the good life stems from recent psychological investigations. Almost everyone assumes that levels of pleasure can be drastically increased, transforming the quality of life, if only one plays one's cards right (or gets lucky). But psychological evidence suggests that, by and large, people "adapt" to new circumstances of life, however more favorable they are. This involves changes in the baseline of what is taken as normal, above which something will seem pleasant. In other words, once people get used to having more, it will take more to please them. Once they get used to having less, it will take less to please them.

When adaptation has taken place, a person's level of subjective well-being (roughly, how pleased the person is) tends to go back to about what it had been. Psychologists have spoken of a "hedonic treadmill," comparing many kinds of human pleasure-seeking with the activity of a hamster or gerbil on its wheel, running hard but getting nowhere.

The classic example presents someone who likes wine, and suddenly is able to afford really fine wine. At first this would be extremely pleasant. But the evidence is that after a while (when really fine wine has become the norm), the increase in the level of wine-drinking pleasure will not be so great.

The most convenient single source for getting a sense of this, and of related recent psychological research, is a collection edited by Daniel Kahneman, Ed Diener, and Norbert Schwartz: *Well-Being: The Foundations of Hedonic Psychology*. The phenomena of adaptation, and the attendant adjustments in subjective well-being levels, have led to attempts to place the data in a theoretical framework. In addition, Kahneman and others have provided an interesting account of distortions in remembered and in anticipated levels of subjective well-being.

Studies document the tendency of subjective well-being levels, after a while, to go back to roughly what had been normal for the individuals concerned. The most dramatic are of lottery winners, and, on the negative side, people who early in life had been rendered paraplegic.[9] There are some exceptions to this tendency, and we shortly will examine what they might point to. The data however suggest that at least some of the most obvious strategies for drastically improving the balance of pleasures over pains, such as getting a lot of money, are highly unlikely to work as well in the longer run as people usually suppose.

This is linked to the distortions, already mentioned, in remembered and anticipated levels of subjective well-being. The data suggest that, say, in remembering how bad a painful experience over a period of time was, people tend to be influenced chiefly by two factors: how bad it was at its peak, and how bad it was at its end. Duration does not seem to be a major factor. One odd result shows that prolonging a painful experience by adding a period of only slight additional pain at the end causes the experience to be remembered as less painful than otherwise would be the case.

Kahneman suggests that the levels of subjective well-being that people anticipate tend to be heavily influenced by a view of the transition (e.g., how it will feel in the weeks after you have won the lottery), and not of the longer run.[10] In the longer run, the levels will not be so different from what you have now. Focusing on the transition period aids the well-known tendency of hope to triumph over experience, in many areas of life.

Much of this goes against what most of us want to believe. It makes the pursuit of greater pleasure, and perhaps of greater happiness, look as if often it contains a delusive element. As Diener and Lucas remark, "It appears that pleasant emotions, the experience of unpleasant emotions and life satisfaction often depend more on temperament than on one's life circumstances or on momentary factors."[11]

Here, as with the Buddhist arguments against strategies of pleasure enhancement, we might wonder whether there are loopholes. Even if

9. See P. Brickman, D. Coates, and R. Janoff-Bulman, "Lottery Winners and Accident Victims: Is Happiness Relative?," in *Journal of Personality and Social Psychology* 37 (1978), 917–27.

10. Daniel Kahneman, "Objective Happiness," in Kahneman et al., eds., *Well-Being: The Foundations of Hedonic Psychology* (New York: Russell Sage Foundation, 1999), 16.

11. See Diener and Lucas, "Personality and Subjective Well-Being," in *Well-Being,* p. 314. There is a complication here in interpreting the psychological evidence, which will be discussed in the Appendix, Number 7.

some of the most obvious strategies for drastically improving the balance of pleasure over pain work only for a short time, might there be anything that works and continues to work? Common sense suggests that changes in the circumstances of life that involve such things as more interesting and challenging activities, or different kinds of human relationships, are candidates. Acquiring and then using the skills that lead to Csikszentmihilyi's "flow" experiences is a strong candidate.

A more general idea might be useful. Barbara Frederickson, in commenting on the data that show that subjective well-being at the peak and at the end dominate one's remembered impression of an experience, suggests that peaks and ends "earn their privileged status because they carry more personal meaning than other moments."[12] Increased pleasures related to sense of self above all carry personal meanings. Perhaps they are not subject to the hedonic treadmill in the same way as pleasures that are not related to sense of self?

This might help to account for the fact that the felt satisfaction (including pleasure in the results) of people who have had plastic surgery tends to remain higher than previously, and in this is exempt from the hedonic treadmill.[13] Some readers may be surprised by this, because they associate plastic surgery with trivial changes of appearance. This popular perspective seems unfair in cases in which the changes are not trivial. But, apart from that, if it does make people feel better about themselves, it has a stronger connection with sense of self than is true for most ordinary pleasures.

The "flow" experiences (of being caught up in exercise of skills) reported by Csikszentmihalyi's subjects also can be related to sense of self, especially when there is room to be proud of the skills involved. Might the quality of close personal relations also give rise to pleasures closely related to sense of self? Certainly many people's lives give that impression. It could be argued that social networks play a major role in our sense of who we are, but that in the West an individualist ideology blinds many people to that fact.[14] It also should be emphasized that many pleasures are augmented if they are shared with people we like.

---

12. Barbara Frederickson, "Extracting Meaning from Past Affective Experiences: The Importance of Peaks, Ends, and Specific Emotions," *Cognition and Emotion* 14 (2000), 589.

13. Frederick and Loewenstein, "Hedonic Adaptation," in *Well-Being,* 313.

14. There are two separate but closely related problems about the self here, which will be discussed in the Appendix, Number 8.

Let me sum up where our discussion of pleasures has left us. Pleasure scores high as a factor in the good life, in terms of our typical motivations, and much less high in terms of people's judgments of how good their lives are at various moments. Human life is full of ambivalence; one root is that two principal sources of our views of what is worth having in life (our desires, and our experience of what it is like to have or to lack something) often point in different directions.

Our motivations often are associated with a feeling that, with luck, we could drastically increase the pleasantness of our lives. The evidence is that the most common ideas of how this might happen are largely based on an illusion, and create a pattern in life of desire and frustration. Actual experience over a period of time can teach us this. But it is a problem that, by the time we have had the necessary experience, habits of desire and pleasure-seeking will be deeply entrenched.

Plato's arguments that some pleasures are worth a lot more than others look strong. Trivial pleasures can be quite nice, but it is not easy to defend parity for them with the pleasures associated with highly meaningful achievements. It remains debatable whether sadistic pleasures, taken in themselves (apart from the pains of victims), can be assigned any positive value.

The pleasures that most arguably have significant value are those associated with the exercise of skills or with forms of personal relations, and these also look less likely than most to exemplify the hedonic treadmill. Hence the idea that levels of pleasure in life can be enhanced for more than a brief period, and introduce greater value into life, is not a complete mistake. But it turns out not to be as easy, and perhaps not as subject to luck, as many people want to believe. Further, it looks as if the values of such a pleasure-enhanced life would have a great deal to do, not merely with the pleasure, but also with the values of the activities that give the pleasure.

To sum up: there is no suggestion in the discussion thus far that pleasures are generally valueless. Nor is there a denial that some of them sometimes are very nice. But there is an argument against any view that the most rewarding kind of life involves the maximum of pleasure, and that this is what we should seek.

The argument is two-pronged. The first suggests that the normal strategies for attempting to maximize pleasure turn out not to be workable, and hence even if maximizing pleasure would be good, it cannot be achieved in the way in which most people think. The second prong is that, in any case, the rewarding life cannot be equated with one that has the maximum of pleasure. This is because the values of pleasures vary enormously, and it is possible to seek pleasures whose value is slight. This argument can be summarized as follows.

A. 1. (The Buddhist Argument) Pleasures are most enjoyed when they are not always easy and immediate. Therefore a high degree of pleasure requires that sometimes there is waiting and difficulty. These involve frustration. Hence a high degree of pleasure entails a high degree of pain (either in frustration beforehand or in boredom afterwards before new desires form). Further, the circumstances of human life are such that over time pain can come to predominate in the life of the avid pleasure-seeker. Hence the normal strategies for attempting to maximize pleasure generally do not work.

2. (The Argument from Recent Psychological Research) Often changes in life that would seem likely to increase drastically the level of pleasure in a life (e.g., winning a lottery) turn out to have this effect only for a limited period of time. After a while it simply takes more to please the newly fortunate person, and levels of satisfaction return to pretty much what they had been. Hence normal strategies for attempting to maximize pleasure generally do not work.

B. Apart from this, there is an argument that not all pleasures are alike in value, and that there can be wide variation. A philosophical form of the argument is found in Plato's *Philebus,* especially in his thought experiment in which you imagine having a choice between the not entirely pleasant human life you presently have and that of a clam in a continuing state of ecstasy. Most people would not make this trade. There is also evidence in Csikszentmihalyi's *Flow: The Psychology of Optimal Experience* that the pleasures most valued are those of losing oneself in skilled activities, and that much more passive pleasures (such as watching television) cumulatively are not experienced as entirely positive. It has been suggested that pleasures that we continue to value are those related to sense of self, which would include those of skilled activities and also those of deep interpersonal relations.

The second prong of this argument leads beyond pleasure in the search for factors that can determine the value found within a life. Of course pleasure matters, but it seems to matter most when what the pleasure is in turns out to be important and deeply connected with your sense of your own life. If we find pleasure in meaningful activities, it seems arbitrary and doctrinaire to assign all of the value to the pleasure and none of it to the activities.

This last point should be spelled out. Csikszentmihalyi's research shows that the experiences that are valued most highly (a valuation that most people on reflection would agree is correct) involve a complex connection among a number of elements. There are the skilled activities, which are the cause and object of pleasure. There also is the losing oneself in these activities, which makes the satisfaction seem both deep and personal. Then of course there is the pleasure.

An obvious point is that if there were no pleasure, the experience would seem very different, and its value would be diminished. This makes it tempting to hold (as John Stuart Mill does seem to) that pleasure is *the* crucial element in value. However, we could equally well say that if no skilled activities were involved, and the pleasure was in something else (say, random sadistic acts), the value would seem negligible. Because of this, it seems arbitrary and doctrinaire to pick out the pleasure element in the complex Csikszenhihalyi describes and to assign all of the value to it.

It also would be counterproductive to focus on the pleasure in what we seek and (if we are fortunate) experience. People lose themselves in activities that they care about. To focus on the element of pleasure is to pull ourselves away from caring about the activities, or the people or things that they connect us with.

## Comfort

Some of the discussion of pleasure should have prepared us for comfort. We have seen that the very strong built-in motivation for enhanced pleasure typically far outweighs its actual role in experiences of subjective well-being. Further, it is clear that most of the pleasures that people ordinarily crave have very slight relation to sense of self, and that one typically adapts to an increased level of such pleasures (so that the level of felt well-being tends to go back to roughly what it had been). Comforts also have typically a minimal relation to sense of self, and are very subject to the process of adaptation.

What is comfort? It is something that can be felt (especially when you are not used to it). But most fundamentally, it is the absence or elimination of something: of bother, minor unpleasant feelings, or of the need to adjust to something. Great comfort is associated with a life made easy.

Once we are thoroughly used to comfort, it is not much felt. When the comfort is new to us, it can provide satisfaction by way of contrast with alternative experiences. Context and the strength of contrast will have a role in whether this occurs. Thus, say, comfortable shoes and clothing, if they are new to us, can feel wonderful. When they are almost always worn, they are not likely to provide felt satisfaction. Rather they will become a baseline for what is viewed as normal, opening the door to feelings of discomfort when less comfortable shoes and clothing are put on. If, on the other hand, comfortable shoes or clothing are worn only infrequently (and much less comfortable shoes or clothing are worn often), their being comfortable will be directly experienced as a kind of pleasure.

There are many comforts that tend to be steady-state, such as those provided by air conditioning in summer and warm rooms in winter. Such comforts, once they have been adjusted to and can be expected, are unlikely to give much in the way of pleasure. They do however create a vulnerability (when systems fail) to discomfort that amounts to noticeable displeasure.

If we ask how much value or importance in a life sensuous comfort of the sort under discussion holds, it is difficult to find a basis for any general answer. It is implausible to suppose that mild discomfort, as represented by rooms that are a bit too warm in summer and a bit too cold in winter, or by shoes that more or less fit but occasionally pinch, will significantly mar anyone's life; in many cases it would be implausible to speak of negative on-line (i.e., able to be felt) affect. Very great discomfort—especially for someone who is not used to it—is much more likely to be marked by negative on-line affect. Also it often can be distracting enough to qualify or preempt any positive experiences one might have. One could imagine a life of ongoing discomfort in which a period of sensuous comfort might seem a real bright spot, one to be remembered for some time afterwards, which would contribute something to the life. For someone whose level of sensuous comfort is steadily high, on the other hand, the comfort would be like emotional wallpaper and arguably would contribute nothing.

Psychic comfort is somewhat like sensuous comfort in offering dwindling satisfaction if it is steady. Some political leaders, it has been claimed, insist on the comfort of being surrounded by advisors whose mindsets and opinions are very like their own. There are analogues to this in academic and everyday life. Clearly there are risks in all of these cases of lack of stimulation and habitual closed-mindedness. On the other hand, some sets of ideas are not likely to be developed in a rich and complex way except through exchanges with people who share some of their starting points, so that in this way a lack of psychic comfort that is both severe and steady also can have its costs.

This said, occasional or low-level psychic discomfort can be highly conducive both to alertness and to openness of mind. Perhaps even extreme psychic discomfort can play a positive role in some kinds of creative work. The discomfort of the unsolved problem can move the investigation forward. It should be admitted that philosophy has an special affinity with discomfort. Good philosophy should make its readers uncomfortable.

What the positive or negative value of comfort or discomfort is in a life depends heavily, it should be said again, on context and elements of contrast. There is much to indicate that a continuous high level of psychic comfort is highly likely to detract from the quality of a life, in part by diminishing the chances for interesting and satisfying creative activity. But a continuous high level of psychic discomfort also can subtract from the quality of life. Here, and in the territory between great comfort and great discomfort, much depends on the circumstances and peculiarities of the individual case.

A third kind of comfort fits under the heading of convenience. Emblematic are the comforts represented by the garage door opener and the television remote control. Both save time, and simplify life slightly by reducing the motion required to get certain things done. Neither would normally provide sensuous satisfaction. There might be pleasure for someone who is not used to them, or for someone who continued to be fascinated by the operation of the device or gladdened by the thought of possessing it. One presumes that for most people this pleasure would wear off very quickly, so that they (like other steady comforts) would take on a wallpaper-like status.

When people talk about "the comforts of home," much of what they typically have in mind must be conveniences; although in some cases warm rooms, comfortable chairs, and showers that work may play a part. Why is home so comfortable for so many? There is the convenience of knowing where everything—well, almost everything—is located, of being able in the morning to reach appropriately for a light switch without having to think.

Much of the trivial business of life can be transacted on, as it were, auto-pilot. Familiarity here has much of the effect (of saving time and effort) that the electronic processing of the garage door opener or TV remote has.

Not only can such comforts save time, but they quicken the subjective pace of felt time. Someone returning from a week of highly eventful travel can feel as if weeks had elapsed, whereas an uneventful week in entirely familiar surroundings can feel as if it had been only a few days. One hypothesis is that events, especially those that require conscious mental orientation, are markers of the passage of time. To have fewer such events means that subjective time speeds up.

Ellen Langer's research in nursing homes suggests also that there may be a correlation between some kinds of comfort (including perhaps the kind under discussion) and the progress of mental debility among the elderly.[15] She was able to increase psychic acuity in her subjects by getting them out of grooves and entrenched patterns of thought, asking them, for example, to provide a story to fit "The early worm gets the bird." Perhaps having to think in the morning about where the light switch is might have a tiny effect of this sort? It is striking also that some of Langer's materials so much resemble Zen puzzles (koans), in that they are crafted so as to require improvisation or rethinking rather than some rote familiar answer.

The tendency of our discussion thus far is to suggest that a steady high level of comfort may be hazardous (at least to psychic acuity), and is not likely to be experientially satisfying. At best it becomes like emotional wallpaper. At worst, it creates a vulnerability to negative experiences when systems fail, a vulnerability made worse by the fact that steady comfort sometimes can weaken people's ability to improvise in difficult situations.

## Conclusion

How important then are pleasure and comfort to the good life? The arguments of this chapter indicate that there is no simple answer. The fact that the great majority of people want more pleasure and more

---

15. For a comprehensive summary of the research, see Ellen Langer, *Mindfulness* (Reading, Mass.: Addison Wesley, 1989).

comfort has to be balanced against the roles that pleasure and comfort actually play in our lives, once we get them. Both the Buddhist argument against pleasure, and the psychological evidence of the hedonic treadmill, show that what we want in the way of providing pleasure very often will not—if we get it—make the positive difference in our lives that we assume it would. Similarly, greater levels of comfort will be satisfying at first, but rapidly will become zero points on our scale of gratifications. In both cases there also are risks: the risk of suffering as we become addicted to desire for pleasure, and the risk of closed-mindedness and dwindling mental acuity that especially attends great psychological comfort.

On the other hand, values of pleasure and comfort cannot be dismissed across the board. Pleasure typically encourages us to continue, or to repeat, whatever gives us pleasure. If the source of pleasure is something worthwhile, then this is a positive role in the direction of our lives. More generally, there is a sense in which (as Aristotle and others have pointed out) pleasure completes the experience of a pleasant activity. If pleasure is absent, this strongly indicates a kind of defect in our involvement in the activity. If we try to imagine a life almost entirely devoid of pleasure, it will look like a life in which activities are consistently flawed or in which we cannot be wholehearted about what we do.

Similarly, an almost entire absence of comfort looks likely to have strongly negative qualities. It can engross a person's awareness, and distract her or him from what would be more meaningful activities. Certainly it generally helps, if someone is about to do something that is important and worth doing, that she or he is reasonably comfortable.

All of this leaves us with a moderate view of the values of pleasure and comfort. It also leaves us with a divided picture of the processes of human nature. Perhaps it is human nature to want more pleasure and more comfort. But it is also part of human nature to develop the capacity for reflective judgment of what one wants. This reflective judgment should yield a mixed picture, highly dependent on the circumstances, of the desirability of more pleasure or of more comfort.

Is there a positive message here, that can aid in the direction of a life? Certainly even a moderate number of small pleasures can enhance a life. This is especially true of pleasures of spontaneity, which can have a special charm.

There is also this. Pleasures of skilled activity, or in general pleasures that are linked to your sense of self (which include those grounded in personal relations), make a more substantial contribution to life than do casual pleasures linked to money and consumption. They are worth working for, although the best strategy is to focus more on activities that are deeply satisfying than on the pleasure they provide.

# Myth Two

## THE DESIRABLE LIFE EQUALS THE ONE THAT IS MOST HAPPY

The last chapter argued that common strategies to maximize pleasure are generally ineffective, and that to equate a highly rewarding life with one that has great pleasure and comfort is unacceptable. Pleasures vary greatly in value; a crucial variable being the value of the activities from which pleasure is derived. Hedonism is a simple view, but it turns out to be too simple. It is tempting then to look for a less simple alternative.

Many people would say that the most rewarding life would be the one with the most happiness. The happiness that everyone (or virtually everyone) wants is a global positive sense about one's life (rather than having as its object some particular thing or experience). Does this happiness always have high value? It might seem at first that this is guaranteed by the nature of happiness.

Happiness is an emotional state that involves tendencies to feel good most of the time. But it also includes a disposition to judge one's life positively. Someone who sincerely says, "My life is wonderful—just what I want it to be" would normally be considered happy, unless there were contrary evidence of, say, hidden distress. So it looks like there is no logical distance between the fact that Bloggs is happy and the judgment that Bloggs is having a good life.

But the most this shows is that there is no logical distance between Bloggs' happiness and Bloggs' judgment that his life is good. Yes, if Bloggs is happy then he is committed to something like the judgment that his life is good. (Maybe all he is committed to is the judgment that it is better than it might have been?) But that does not commit anyone else to a positive judgment of the quality of Bloggs' life.

It would not go against logic for the rest of us to think that the life about which Bloggs is happy is actually crummy and inadequate and could be better. We could be wrong. Perhaps we all missed subtle features of his life that are meaningful and have great value. Also, the fact that Bloggs *feels* happy surely should count for something.

Judgments from the outside could be correct, however, even if they differ from the judgment implicit in the happiness of the person whose life it is. Imagine someone who as a result of an accident undergoes a right side frontal lobotomy (and then is reduced to a state of idiocy and is happy as a clam). We should be sorry for the victim, even if he or she is very happy. Such a person has less of a life than would have seemed possible. The life of an idiot who is happy is certainly better than that of an idiot who is not happy, but still it is not much of a life.

Hence happiness is not everything. Sometimes it may not be worth much. Other things (such as being an active, intelligent person) can matter more.

Even if this argument is valid, it may be hard to shake the feeling that something is missing. Is it simply that one of our stock ideas, of which we cannot easily get free, is that happiness is the essential personal goal in life? Or is there something about happiness and its link with what is desirable in life that we have not properly explored? We need to look more closely at what makes happiness the primary magnet, for philosophers and nonphilosophers alike, in thinking about what makes life worth living.

## The Pursuit of Happiness

The American Declaration of Independence affirms a universal right to "life, liberty, and the pursuit of happiness." The way the wording swerves when it reaches "happiness" is intriguing. Why not affirm a right to "life, liberty, and happiness"?

There is no entirely adequate short answer. Governments in fact can protect the life, liberty, and happiness of their citizens. We can see that happiness needs to be protected because that of most or all happy people can be ruined under suitably adverse conditions. The death or removal of family members, sudden extreme impoverishment, or severe chronic disease can ruin happiness.[1] Hence happiness appears to be roughly on the same plane as life and liberty, at least as regards the protective functions of governments.

There may seem to be more of a difference if we look at how happiness (as opposed to life and liberty) is created. Short of compulsory right side frontal lobotomies or mood-altering drugs in the drinking water, governments cannot make people happy. Life and liberty are givens in the right kind of society. But happiness is never a given. You have to get it for yourself. Hence "the pursuit of happiness."

This is a start. But we can get at the peculiarity of happiness better if we look further at its individualized character. It is notorious that the kind of thing that would make one person happy might well not make another happy. The pursuit of happiness, therefore, does not really consist of all of us scrambling toward the same goal. Also, most of us may not be at all sure what would make us happy. Perhaps what works in the short run might not work in the long run? Because of this, the search for happiness involves a good deal more than merely moving toward a target. There also is a process of figuring out what the goals should be.

What we have seen already about the compound nature of happiness suggests that the figuring out will have more aspects than we might have thought. Happiness is an emotional state over a period of time of mainly feeling good. One of its elements is a disposition to judge positively the general character of one's life. Hence, figuring out what would give you happiness has at least two aspects. One is the attempt to find out what would give you the overarching emotional state, with its preponderance of feeling good, that is characteristic of happiness. Another is reflection on the kind of life available to you that you would consider desirable.

For most people this is a single, seamless process. But certainly tensions between the two main components are possible. Mabel may be inclined to feel that activities that lead to her feeling good over a period of time are somehow unworthy. She can be happy only if the thought of unworthiness does not surface at all often. Conversely, George can be convinced that only a life of a certain sort (say, one of strenuous socially responsible

---

1. These brief remarks on vulnerability need much more comment. Some philosophies have suggested ways in which we can be largely, or perhaps entirely, invulnerable. See the Appendix, Number 9.

activity) is worthwhile, but finds that it simply does not give him a pre-ponderance of feeling good.

Perhaps "the heart has reasons that the reason knows not," not only in religion (as the seventeenth-century French philosopher Blaise Pascal said) but also in the conduct of life. Chapter 4 will explore the ramifications of this. But even if this is so, we should not automatical-ly assume that reasons "of the heart" are the best ones. Someone who drifts into a life of extreme greed, causing other people to suffer, may feel that occasional (troubling and depressing) thoughts such as "This is irresponsible" should give way to the inner direction of his or her urges. There is certainly a strong case for regarding this as a mistake. It is arguably a mistake of two kinds. It is a moral mistake to build a life on the suffering of other people. But arguably also such a life will not be as rewarding and worth leading as the person who pursues it might like to think.

Let us review the main components of personal happiness. The first is what you find makes you feel good over a period of time. The other is reflective judgments of what would give you the best quality of life. My suggestion is that it would be unreasonable to give either one of these sources precedence over the other, across the board, in all cases.

Ideas about what is most desirable in life may conflict with what you actually do desire—something that could be fairly good, and for which one is best suited. (Perhaps you should give up the idea that your life is wasted if you do not pursue career X, and instead take up the career that actually appeals more?) Or yours could be a case of sound judgments about quality of life telling you that your unrealistic urges lead in an ulti-mately undesirable direction. (You keep desiring to do X, but no reason-able person would believe that it would work for you.) We cannot rule out either possibility, which is one reason why such conflicts are so diffi-cult. They are difficult also because, unless they are resolved, the person who has them cannot be happy.

A government that is not intolerably intrusive cannot help you with such issues. At best, if you settle on what you think is a path to happiness, it can remove obstacles and provide opportunities. This is an important truth about governments and their limitations. But it connects also with an important truth about happiness: that its precise form is indeterminate, with a content that varies from person to person, and frequently can be problematic for an individual.

## Vectors of Happiness

Much of the discussion up to now has been predicated on the apparent fact that what makes someone happy varies from person to person, so that part of the pursuit of happiness is arriving at a better sense of what is likely to make you happy. Are there no useful generalizations at all about what leads to happiness? A short answer is that there are some, mainly statistical but some connected with major areas of life related to happiness. A good source is Michael Argyle's *The Psychology of Happiness*. Another, also sophisticated and highly reliable yet more informal, is Martin Seligman's *Authentic Happiness*.

Both books have to deal (as this one is doing) with the fact that it is difficult to arrive at many generalizations that are both sweeping and valid about what is most important in happiness, or in a life good enough that one should be happy about it. The difficulty lies in the variations of individual lives, but also in the fact that features important in some lives can be subtle and difficult to articulate.

Seligman at one point lists six core virtues endorsed by a variety of major ethical traditions, each of which can be subdivided into a cluster of personal strengths that are conducive to happiness (p. 11). These are wisdom and knowledge, courage, love and humanity, justice, temperance, and spirituality and transcendence. Seligman knows that each of these can take a variety of forms, and that generalization hence requires broad and unspecific labels. It turns out, for example, that transcendence here can include not only the religious sense of a higher or supernatural power, but also (alternatively) an aesthetic response to the world that has some affinities to this (p. 154).

Argyle speaks of happiness "as part of a broader syndrome, which includes choice of rewarding situations, looking at the bright side, and high self-esteem" (p. 124). Like Seligman, Argyle is deft at putting briefly in ordinary English a set of insights that, spelled out, would turn out to be long, complex, and more shapeless than one would have liked. Still the insights should be explored. Let us look at the three elements of his "broader syndrome" of happiness.

First, the choice of rewarding situations is an important determinant of how happy someone will be. The basic insight is that people who are happy by and large avoid (and have avoided) situations that involve unnecessary high risks, or real chances of becoming miserable or of having one's deepest and most enduring desires thwarted. Argyle is almost certainly using "choice" for behavior that could have been different. A choice in this sense does not have to have been deliberate, or even consciously made. Happy people simply tend to gravitate to situations that will bring out their best qualities, or in which they will have a good chance to fulfill themselves. And they tend to gravitate away from situations of opposite sorts.

Of course we often cannot predict with very great confidence what the effect of a situation on us, or on anyone else, will be. So it is possible for basically happy people to get themselves into bad situations. Furthermore, external events and sheer luck can limit options. Sometimes bad situations are not only unforeseeable but also (even if foreseen) unavoidable.

Even when basically happy people get themselves into bad situations, this still leaves the possibility that further choosing within the situations will affect how unfortunate these are as they develop. There is a mental laziness that can make us wish to regard choosing as typically a one-off process in most matters. You make your bed (as the adage has it) and then you lie in it. Often though, choosing is a continuous process. You can monitor what you have been choosing. You then can adjust or drastically change your course, particularly if inner alarms sound.

People can feel that their lives are something that just, as it were, happened to them. Happy people with that view often feel lucky, and unhappy people feel unlucky. But the first of Argyle's three elements suggests that much of this "luck" can amount to poor choices, which may well have not been consciously made. It should be emphasized that this claim does not apply to all of what might seem like luck.

This view pushes the attribution of much of our luck back a step or two, to the childhood acquisition of habits of mind that prepare one for life. The nineteenth-century German philosopher Friedrich Nietzsche said that to be a person of character is to have one's characteristic experience.[2] Whether he was referring to deep psychological luck or to something else, there seems to be much truth in this observation. People who are happy in the long run just do have, by and large, good experiences.

How an experience is taken has a great deal to do with how good it will seem. The second of Argyle's two elements, "Looking at the bright side,"

2. This is my loose translation. Walter Kaufmann translates it in *Beyond Good and Evil*, (New York: Vintage Books, 1989, Epigrams and Interludes No. 70, 80), as "If one has character one also has one's typical experience, which recurs repeatedly."

connects with this. No doubt there are experiences that are thoroughly rotten, in which any discernment of a bright side would be most implausible. But arguably the vast majority of human experiences are complicated and mixed in character, especially considering latent factors that would contribute to a rebound from what an experience mainly represents.

Looking at the bright side undoubtedly contributes to positive affect, enabling us to dwell on aspects of our situation that are appealing. It can make possible a preponderance of good moods, which can matter more to our feeling about life than some pleasures now and then would. But also it can have a causal role in our readiness to reverse whatever are the negative factors in the present experience.

These first two of the three elements in Argyle's "broader syndrome" are causal contributors to people's being happy, at least in part. The third element (along with the aspect of looking at the bright side that contributes to positive affect) is constitutive. That is to say that moderately high self-esteem is part of any happiness. Why is this so? To see why, we need to understand better what is happiness, and what should count as high self-esteem. To understand this matters in the pursuit of happiness, and major educational issues hinge on this understanding.

Recall that the happiness under discussion (the kind that everyone most wants) is a global positive sense about one's life. You can be happy (in a nonglobal sense) about a pay raise, or a grade on an exam, or about a concert you went to. These are very nice emotions to have, but like pleasures they are tied to their objects (to what they are about) and are transitory. Happiness in the global sense is not tied to specific objects and typically is not so transitory. It can last for months, years, or a lifetime.

In a way, happiness is a positive feeling about the world; but at the heart of the view of the world that each of us has, there is a "me" of which we tend to be very aware. If someone does not like her or his "me," that spoils everything. Hence a person's attitude toward herself or himself is a major contributor to (or makes a major subtraction from) happiness. This makes happiness quite different from pleasure.

Pleasures are, at least in the short run, a matter of the luck of the draw—of whether people are lucky enough to get most of what they fancy. If that happens, they will have considerable pleasure (until they "adapt" and the hedonic treadmill begins moving, or until their luck changes—whichever happens first). Happiness of the objectless kind, conversely, is to a large degree a matter of how well you have come to terms with yourself. Someone who basically dislikes himself or herself, then, could have a lot of pleasures next week and still not be happy. You cannot come to terms with yourself unless you accept yourself, to some degree. Hence a moderately high degree of self-esteem.

Self-esteem is sometimes contrasted with self-respect. The latter has to do with two areas of extreme reluctance. Someone who has self-respect will be extremely unwilling to be treated in a degrading or humiliating way. This is linked to a strong sense of having certain basic rights as a rational being. Someone with self-respect also will have certain things that she or he simply would not do because they are unworthy. It might be because they are immoral, have bad manners, or are just plain stupid. Whatever the category, if you have self-respect you normally will not do what you think is unworthy.

One can easily imagine a community in which some are rich and others poor, some are famous and others obscure, in which everyone has approximately equal self-respect. This seems less likely in relation to self-esteem, which has more to do with abilities, successes, and the like; although arguably in many communities virtually everyone has some specific ability that is not very widely shared and can be impressive in its way. To have high self-esteem is to have a strongly positive attitude toward some aspects of who one is (that one also regards as fairly central), and not to have a strongly negative attitude toward any other central aspects. Moderately high self-esteem, which I am suggesting is all that is required for happiness, is to have a positive (although not necessarily uncritical) attitude toward some central aspects of who one is, and not to have a strongly negative attitude toward any other central aspects.

Self-esteem and self-respect can overlap, in that some people can have high self-esteem as a matter of pride in the moral virtue implicit in their self-respect. Conversely, it is hard to see how someone who feels deeply unworthy because of moral failings could have the self-esteem required to be happy. However, there certainly are people whose general behavior seems morally acceptable who all the same are lacking in self-esteem. They know they are not evil, but all the same do not feel positive about themselves. Others, whose moral self-rating is not terribly high, might not be bothered by these moral blemishes and might have high self-esteem based on their performance in other areas of life. Self-esteem or its lack can have many different sources.

Often a person's self-esteem appears to be determined, first, by recognized success in what is required in school, and later by what is normally regarded as success in work and/or family life. First-stage self-esteem thus can be enmeshed in the educational system. This is where educational issues arise. Some educators have made two claims, one of which seems obviously true and the other of which involves some complicated and difficult questions. They have claimed (1) that a sense of succeeding in school promotes self-esteem, and (2) that schools therefore can promote self-esteem by arranging their demands so that every (or virtually every) student succeeds.

One trap in discussions of self-esteem (as in many other areas) is that of viewing what is at stake as a static goal, realizable in the short run and then presumably (at least normally) in perpetuity. Certainly any child who keeps getting a little gold star or a smiley face on her or his work is likely to have some self-esteem. If self-esteem is a static goal, then that child should be set for life.

In the real world that child may be badly prepared for much of life. The world outside of schools will not be so amiable. Indeed, even colleges often turn out not to be as generous as many students would like. Beyond the educational system, jobs are lost, marriages fail, and other bad things happen to amiable people who have a history of little gold stars and smiley faces.

These things happen even to highly competent people who have high self-esteem. As suggested earlier, in any situation (however bad it may look), it usually is the case that further choices are available, so that there will be ways of handling or containing whatever is difficult or disagreeable. Intuitively, it seems clear that practice in this kind of sustained management of what is difficult and disagreeable would be useful, even in a fairly early stage of education. Easy victories do not provide this practice.

High self-esteem founded on easy victories will be highly fragile, and in most normal lives unlikely to last. What replaces it will depend in large part on the individual. In some cases it might be peevishness, or a sense of having been victimized by forces beyond one's control. Whatever it is, it will not be conducive to happiness.

High self-esteem that is tenable in the long run will require a vivid sense that things sometimes do go wrong, and will require a resilience— a willingness to endure patiently and at the same time to work for betterment. An educational system can contribute to this, not by offering easy victories but rather by stage-managing what are likely to be eventual victories in tasks that require patience and skill acquisition.

Having genuine skills that were not easy to acquire and having persisted despite difficulties can be sources of a less fragile self-esteem. Further, the process just described can lead to habits of mind that include resilience and perseverance. These can be invaluable in the rest of life.

Someone who has high self-esteem of the nonfragile sort, who basically likes herself or himself, is likely to be happy. How very happy can depend on other factors, including the texture of personal relationships. This parallels Aristotle's judgment of the *eudaemonia* (sometimes translated as "happiness," but better as "well-being") of King Priam of Troy, whose family and city were destroyed at the end of the Trojan War. His *eudaemonia* (given this disaster) could not be placed at the highest level, but still, Aristotle insisted, could be judged as not negligible.[3]

## Happiness and Comparative Standards

We have already seen some major respects in which happiness of the global kind is a very different kind of thing from pleasure. Here is another. How happy we are can depend very considerably on how we compare our lives to those of others. Consider a comparable phenomenon in relation to pleasures: if other people seem to be getting much more pleasure than you are, you might be inclined to have less interest in getting more of what has been giving you the smaller doses of pleasure. But more often than not, pleasure is simply experienced for what it is, without any pronounced element of comparison to what others have. It is much more common for such comparative elements to enter into assessments of happiness. This may be in part because of the "whole life" aspect of states of global happiness.

Indeed, a keen sense that others are better off—if those others seem in most respects comparable to oneself—can mar someone's happiness. Envy is a large topic in the realm of happiness, although not in the realm of pleasure. Nietzsche regarded envy as a litmus test of the satisfactoriness of a life, and presumably of its genuine happiness. If you envied other people, he thought, this showed that there was something unsatisfactory about the way you were living.

Why are these comparisons—the ones that sometimes can mar happiness —made to the lives of those who seem most like oneself? Presumably the

---

3. Aristotle, *Nicomachean Ethics*, trans. Terence Irwin, Second Edition (Indianapolis: Hackett Publishing Co., 1999), 1101a, 14.

happiness of a peasant in the middle ages rarely was affected by comparison with the lives of the rulers or the nobility. It may be that the lives of people like ourselves give us our sense of what should be possible for us, and perhaps then of what we should expect of ourselves.

This connects with a difficult subject. In a classic work, *The Hidden Injuries of Class,* two sociologists (Sennett and Cobb) examine the psychic wounds of low status workers who feel that they could have done better in life. What is reported is troubling and sad. Comparisons seem to make these workers definitely less happy.

That the comparisons arise and are depressing for some suggests something unpalatable: there could be a negative correlation between freedom of opportunity (something that most of us strongly believe in) and levels of happiness. Perhaps it would be easier to be happy, really happy, in a traditional hierarchical society in which an assigned place awaits you, and there are no dispiriting thoughts of "I could have done better"?

On the other hand, even in a society like ours, there can be personal strategies for lessening the sting of any comparisons with others. A classic strategy is of lowered expectations. Someone who feels prepared for outcomes that are only moderately good at best will be less vulnerable to keen disappointment or invidious comparisons.

This can involve a complex balancing act. Arguably one of the risks of lowered expectations is that confidence—even confidence that is slightly higher than it reasonably should be—can be conducive to achievement. Most of us in fact overestimate our abilities, and perhaps this is in some respects a good thing. Psychological research has disclosed that the one group in the population with a fairly accurate estimate of their own capacities is that of people suffering from severe depression.[4] Perhaps a high level (within limits) of confidence can be conducive to mental health, as well as to achievement. Could a person combine high confidence with lowered expectations?

Not easily. But let me suggest that it is possible, especially for people who have cultivated a wry sense of the tricks that life can play on us. There can be a sense that, even if you do your best—and one's best is

---

4. See Nico Frijda, "Moods, Emotion Episodes, and Emotions," in *Handbook of Emotions,* eds. M. Lewis and J. M. Haviland (New York: Guilford Press, 1993), 396; L. B. Alloy and L. Y. Abramson, "Judgment of Contingency in Depressed and Nondepressed Subjects. Sadder But Wiser?" in *Journal of Experimental Psychology: General* (1979) 108, 441–85.

good—things still might not work out. A heightened form of this sense is close to what the Spanish philosopher Miguel de Unamuno characterized as "the tragic sense of life," something that he thought was widespread among Mediterranean peoples, and not so common in countries like the United States.[5] Someone who has a high level of confidence and can imagine very good outcomes without at all counting on them could do her or his best and could achieve a great deal—while at the same time being prepared for a shrug of the shoulders if things do not work out.

A different version of a complex attitude toward the future, of having it both ways, is found in the classic Indian text the *Bhagavad Gita*. Its central recommendation is that you should train yourself to be able to lose yourself in action, to be carried away in sequences of skilled activities. Crucial to this loss of self in action is that you not have concern about outcomes. You simply carry on in that satisfying way, without having anxious thoughts like "Will we win?" Even so, the sequence of skilled actions is tailored to be effective. Not worrying about outcomes is compatible with not being careless, and with your doing whatever needs to be done.

If it is possible (although it takes a lot of training, and is not easy) to be a high achieving person without concern about outcomes, then it should be possible also to be a high achieving person without giving way to comparisons with other people's lives. Self-discipline is required. But the self-discipline is very much part of any real immersion in skilled activity.

## Happiness and Stability

Life, as we all know, keeps changing. So do we. No one is exactly the same person as she or he was five or ten years ago. Interests and values often change, and patterns of response are subtly altered. Typically there is some continuity, including broad similarities, in this inevitable change. We normally expect some unity in a person's life, some points of connection among the personality structures and the behavior of various stages. This unity is a matter of degree. At one extreme there are people who only barely seem to change the way they think and feel. At the other, there are

5. Miguel de Unamuno, *The Tragic Sense of Life*, trans. J. E. C. Flitch (London: Fontana Books, 1962).

people who are so variable (even within a short time period) that we hardly know who they are.

It is important to maintain a sense of the lack of neatness and the variability here—both of the behavior of many individuals, and of meanings. Both can be heavily dependent on context.[6]

It may well be that happy people can be found both among those whose conduct often varies and among those whose conduct generally does not. One should always be wary of broad generalizations about human life that do not allow for exceptions, which keep cropping up. Let me suggest a weaker kind of generalization. By and large, a fairly high degree of stability in one's nature or character is conducive to happiness.

Here is one reason why this is plausible. We have seen that happiness is based on sense of self to a significant degree, so that one cannot be happy without liking oneself at least somewhat. Self-esteem hence is a major factor. All of this requires, as it were, a target for the essential positive attitude: a self that one can like or think well of. A self that is stable enough

6. As noted in the Introduction, it is a great oversimplification to think that knowledge of an individual's character or of national character allows one to predict with certainty how the individual or nation will behave over time in a variety of situations. This is comparable to the simplifications represented in the six myths of this book—and also to some peculiarly philosophical simplifications, such as assuming that all meaningful utterances are representations of something, or that a word like "game" has a definition that fits all of its uses. Games vary enormously. This is taken up in a slightly comic example of Wittgenstein's philosophical therapy (*Philosophical Investigations*, trans. G. E. M. Anscombe, London: Macmillan, 1953, 33e). He imagines a man asking him to show the children a game, and that he then shows them how to gamble with dice. The man then insists that he did not mean that kind of game. But had this exclusion been in the man's mind? That would be very unlikely. This brief passage is designed to undermine any tendency to think that all games share some essence and are alike. More importantly, it undermines any generalization that meanings are always in the mind, determined by what the speaker has in mind. It is true that there are some cases of ambiguity in which what the speaker or author intended will be treated as decisive. But in cases like the one in which the man asked Wittgenstein to show the children a game, contextual and social factors determine the meaning even if it had not occurred to the man to exclude gambling with dice. The argument for this is not explicit; but if you follow what Wittgenstein is saying (and think about it), you will see something at the end. Context (including social expectations) matters to the meaning of an utterance. It also enters in to the behavior of people we know (and to our own behavior) in various situations, and as it develops through time.

that one can have a sense of its broad tendencies would seem to be a better target.

In fact many people's self-esteem is founded in part on things that they have done well, and probably will continue to do well. Some of these are moral choices. "It was a difficult situation, but I did the right thing" will contribute to self-esteem. But so will nonmoral capacities and achievements. For many people the kind of work they do, or what they do for their families, is crucial to self-esteem. All of this matters more if its base is not something that happens once in a while but rather something that happens (or happened) over a period of time or repeatedly. Even in the moral cases, while the fact that "I did the right thing" will contribute to self-esteem, it will contribute more if there has been a pattern of usually doing the right thing.

Some philosophers have suggested that narrative unity (a sense of a connected story) within a life has a strong connection with a sense of self.[7] Narrative unity is strengthened by continuing purposes or personal relations. But it also is strengthened if there is some continuity of style in dealing with the world, as manifested in good performances.

## Can Someone Be Too Happy?

Much of the discussion thus far has proceeded on two assumptions: (1) that virtually everyone wants to be happy, and (2) that (as virtually everyone believes) happiness is by and large a very good thing. Exceptions to the second claim have been suggested. When happiness is bound up with idiocy, especially in the case of a previously normal person rendered brain-damaged as the result of an accident, it does not look so desirable. Other kinds of cases also look like plausible exceptions to the second claim. These include the lives of people whose happiness is bound up with extremely trivial and limited sets of activities. They also include lives in which the major source of satisfaction is in making other people suffer.

The exceptions can be debated. But my sense is that most readers will find at least one or two of them convincing. This can lead to a

7. See Alasdair MacIntyre, *After Virtue* (Notre Dame: University of Notre Dame Press, 1978), 202ff.

view that happiness is a very good thing, except in cases of certain specified sorts. A natural further thought is that, if in normal cases happiness is very good, then the more of it the better. What follows is an argument against regarding this as always true. It is possible to be too happy.

The points to be made against extreme happiness will divide into two sorts. First we can consider undesirable causal effects, or risks, of extreme happiness. If these exist, then the strongest reasonable claim for extreme happiness would be that—taken in itself—it is desirable, with the concession that considering the risks it perhaps is not to be recommended. Finally there will be a criticism of extreme happiness in itself. If this is accepted, the conclusion would have to be that extreme happiness often is not desirable in itself, as well as often being risky.

First let us characterize extreme happiness. The general discussion of happiness suggests that extreme happiness would have to be complete.[8] It would involve total self-acceptance, self-esteem with no significant qualifications. Of course other factors in life matter to happiness, including one's social relations and work, and such banal matters as financial status, housing, etc. Extreme happiness presumably would involve entire satisfaction with all of these.

Clearly it would feel very nice. In a view of life that allows for a static goal that, once achieved, becomes permanent, it would have to rank very high. Chapter 3 will argue that the idea of a static goal is a mistake, at least for this life. Many readers will immediately think of an afterlife that can be presumed to be static. Let us put to the side though questions about the afterlife, which are essentially religious, and continue to focus on the present life, the one that we are experiencing.[9]

---

8. In what follows I speak interchangeably of extreme and complete happiness. It might be thought that extreme happiness need not be complete: it could be very keen in some areas, even though lacking somewhat in the zone of self-acceptance. There is no doubt that people can be very happy even if they are not completely happy. But the idea of extreme happiness contains the notion of something that verges on a maximum, and this requires completeness.

9. Not all religious accounts of an afterlife portray it as static. Many Asian and classical Greek accounts of reincarnation are obvious exceptions. *The Tibetan Book of the Dead* is an especially elaborate exception, in that it focuses on decisions you will make after you are dead (although you may not realize that you are dead). Within Christian accounts of varieties of afterlife, the one that involves purgatory is nonstatic.

A classical view suggests that extreme happiness is dangerous in this life. It is brought out, in Herodotus' *History* by the story of King Croesus (a wealthy ruler in Asia Minor), who thought that he was the happiest of men. He is admonished by an Athenian visitor, Solon, that such judgments are best postponed until the end of life. He recalls this admonition when he is defeated by the Persians and is about to be executed. Even though his life is then spared, it is clear that he will never again think that he is extremely happy.

Solon's main point was that the proper domain of a judgment of happiness is a whole life, and that you cannot be sure of the character of the whole life until it is at its end. However, then as now people must have sometimes described themselves as being happy; it is hard to believe that Solon would have strenuously objected if Croesus had merely remarked that he was happy. Indeed, Solon speaks of some men as having, in the course of their lives, "a gleam of happiness."[10] Croesus slipped into a double error: claiming that he was superlatively happy, and treating this as if it were a definitive and fixed truth about his life.

To have these thoughts is to be entirely unguarded, and to be vulnerable to problems and difficulties to which a less thoroughly happy person would be alert. We need to be mindful of the fact that the world keeps changing and difficulties arise. People who do not have the false sense of security that feeling superlatively happy brings will be better able to cope with the difficulties. If they lacked the false sense of security, on the other hand—if they were aware of risks and vulnerability—they still could be happy, but not be superlatively happy.

All of this is common sense. Another factor emerges in Herodotus, a belief about the order of the world that includes the assumption that the world tends to bounce back from extremes. Consider the following story. Polycrates (another ancient ruler) had extremely good luck in life for some time. His friend and ally warns him that perpetual good fortune is dangerous, and suggests that he modify his good fortune by throwing away something he especially values. Polycrates follows the advice and throws a valuable ring into the sea. But five or six days later he is given a newly caught fish, and the ring is in its stomach. This is yet more good fortune. When he tells his friend of it, his friend knows that he is doomed,

---

10. *The History of Herodotus*, trans. George Rawlinson (New York: Tudor Books, 1934), Book I, 12.

and edges away so as not to share the grief. Indeed Polycrates is doomed; soon after, his realm is conquered and he is killed.[11]

There may be something to this, and it could be given a naturalistic explanation. Good luck in what is genuinely a matter of luck is never constant. Even if much that seems like "luck" is shaped by the person who has it, there is such a thing as sheer luck. Whether rain spoils a picnic whose date was set far in advance, for example, is not shaped by any of the people involved.

Sheer luck is never constant. We all know this, and speak of "the law of averages." But people who have had a run of really good luck sometimes forget this. This makes them extremely vulnerable, especially because any learned extreme optimism can breed carelessness. Hence the bad things that happened to Polycrates in the end should not surprise us.

Thus far we have seen that complete happiness can contribute to personal vulnerability, at the very least because of the lack of wariness and recognition of risk factors it is likely to engender. Consider another complaint along these lines against the ideal of extreme or complete happiness. Many people have suggested that the best kind of happiness is that linked to personal achievement. Part of the idea is that there would be something of real value to justify someone's being positive about her or his life in such cases. But it can be argued that extreme happiness (as opposed to, say, moderate happiness) is not conducive to significant achievements.

The phrase "significant achievements" is used here broadly. I am not referring merely to such successes as making a scientific discovery or creating a very good work of art. Creating a successful family life, with happy and productive children, is a major achievement. So is contributing significantly to a harmonious and satisfying workplace, or to effective institutions that do some good. There are very many varieties of significant achievements. They share two qualities. One is that they do some good. The other is that they are not easy, and typically in fact require sustained activity. If something were done easily, in the twinkling of an eye, we usually would not regard it as a significant achievement. An exception to this would be the case in which the quick and easy achievement was the result of really unusual skills, and typically such skills require some sustained effort either to acquire or to maintain. There is thus a strong connection—

11. Ibid., Book III, 161–92.

general although perhaps not absolutely invariable—between significant achievement and sustained effort.

Sustained effort normally requires either a sense that things are not entirely as they should be, or that there is a risk that they might become not entirely as they should be. It would be very hard to be superlatively happy if one thought with some care about these risks, or about ways in which things are not entirely as they should be. Hence superlative happiness is far from conducive to significant achievement. If the suggestion above—that the best kind of happiness is linked to personal achievement —is correct, it will also be the case that superlative happiness is not the best kind of happiness.

To avoid misunderstanding, let me say that there is no suggestion here that it is somehow in general better to be unhappy. Perhaps there are some conditions in life so unacceptable that only someone thoroughly unhappy with them will be able to accomplish their removal. In such cases, unhappiness might be conducive to significant achievement. But common experience suggests that moderately happy people often make significant achievements in various areas of life. Where personal relations are a factor especially, the (moderate) happiness of the agent could make a big positive difference in what could be achieved. In many areas of endeavor, also, personal unhappiness can be simply a distraction.

The tendency of much of this chapter can be put crudely. If a psychologist asks you to rate how happy you are, on a scale of one up to seven, perhaps the ideal setting on the happiness meter would be a six. Of course it would be ridiculous to suppose that we really can be *precise* about how happy a person is, and one can be confident that no reputable psychologist believes otherwise. Also in practice the ideal setting might vary with aspects of a person's life that justify happiness. The sadist, for example, *should* be unhappy. My point simply is this: complete happiness is by and large not to be recommended, but (subject to some exceptions) a moderately high degree of happiness is.

Thus far the argument against complete happiness has concentrated on causal connections, on the risk factors associated with it. We can now look at the intrinsic features of complete happiness. This will lead to an argument that it is not to be recommended, even discounting causal connections.

Recall that complete happiness would require entire satisfaction with all of the significant factors in one's life (family life, other personal relations, career, housing, financial status, etc.) and also total self-acceptance (self-esteem with no significant qualifications). For reasons that will become apparent, it is important to keep separate these two compartments of what underlies extreme happiness (the self, and everything that surrounds or connects with the self). We can look at them one at a time.

Many people's first reaction might be to think that entire satisfaction with everything that surrounds or connects with the self would be a sign either of limited intelligence or of willful blindness. Of course, they will say, we live in an imperfect world. It is perhaps not sheer idiocy to think that everything about it is entirely satisfactory. But it can verge on idiocy. Further, while we are here on earth, it is important that we try to make things better, and to prevent them from getting worse. An attitude of entire satisfaction is not conducive to real effort in this.

There may well be something to this line of thought. But there is one form of entire satisfaction with everything that surrounds or connects with us that seems to me very able to be defended against this criticism. This is the idealized perfect religious faith examined by the Danish philosopher Soren Kierkegaard in *Fear and Trembling.* As Kierkegaard describes it, someone who was totally convinced that every detail of the universe was managed by a perfect being might still have his or her preferences—even in such banal details as what food would be available for dinner—but would be perfectly happy with whatever then happened, because it was God's will.

In Kierkegaard's presentation, entire acceptance of the world around one is still compatible with real effort to shape it as one prefers. The effort makes sense because it too is willed by God. If one's efforts in the end do not succeed, then this too is God's will and hence entirely acceptable. Perhaps the one major qualification that attends this account of what perfect faith would be (a qualification that Kierkegaard would readily accept) is that it goes far beyond the set of attitudes held by the vast majority of people who are normally considered religious. It certainly is not an easy option.

However it does suggest a possible case in which someone could have entire acceptance of the surrounding world, one that is compatible with high intelligence and also conducive to efforts to change factors in the surrounding world. Kierkegaard also creates a plausible case for holding that someone who is entirely satisfied with God's management of the world could have an enviable set of life experiences. All in all, it may begin to look as if his version of what perfect faith would be involves an extreme happiness that in itself (and also in its causal connections) is entirely acceptable.

My reading of Kierkegaard suggests though that the case he presents is not one of what I have termed extreme or complete happiness, and is not intended to be. The title of his examination of faith, *Fear and Trembling,* is a good clue. To reach the attitude of perfect faith that he recommends would involve real strain, and to maintain it also would be difficult. The perfect faith, he says, requires a double movement; half of it is infinite resignation, with which the knight of faith "has drained the cup of life's profound sadness."[12] The entire acceptance of the world, in short, has to involve a tension within the self.

The general picture of ourselves and our universe that Kierkegaard presupposes (a picture which to some degree is shared by most forms of Christianity, Judaism, and Islam) leaves little or no room for criticism of events in the universe; after all, they represent decisions of a wise deity. But it also holds that this wise deity created a universe in which (for inscrutable divine purposes) a collection of spiritually imperfect beings (i.e., humans) was included. Someone who entirely accepts this picture can be in a way entirely satisfied with what happens in the universe, but also will have an undertow of "profound sadness." There also might well be a lack of entire satisfaction with one's imperfect self. This combination very likely would involve being happier than most people, especially in that the despair that Kierkegaard maintains plagues the vast majority of people would be eliminated. But it would not add up to what I have called extreme happiness.

In short, even if you admire Kierkegaard's ideal of life, it does not provide (and I think is not intended to provide) a counter-argument to the criticism of complete happiness that is underway. Nor does, I think, any other religious ideal, however attractive it may be. Some might think of the classic Buddhist portrayal of the enlightened person, near to nirvana, who has achieved a kind of personal perfection and is impervious to suffering no matter what happens in the world. In this case it seems a misreading to suppose that the ideal is in any way about happiness. Most translations into English use words such as "bliss" or "joy," both of which

---

12. See Soren Kierkegaard, *Fear and Trembling* and *The Sickness Unto Death*, trans. Walter Lowrie (Princeton: Princeton University Press, 1969), 51, also 58.

are quite different from happiness (even though all three are positive emotional states). It would have seemed very odd, and entirely out of character, if Buddha had said "I'm very happy." Really, what is promised to an enlightened person is a very different kind of inner glow, beyond the dimension of happiness and unhappiness.

An element that should be present in the life of an intelligent, moderately happy person is the capacity for self-criticism. This element is entirely compatible with Kierkegaard's ideal of perfect faith. It is irrelevant to Buddha's ideal, in that at a certain point the enlightened follower of Buddha is supposed to realize fully that she or he has no self (and in that sense nothing to criticize). The capacity for self-criticism is incompatible with a standing sense of total self-acceptance that amounts to self-esteem with no significant qualifications. There have to be significant qualifications in self-esteem, areas in which you are not sure that all of your attitudes and tendencies are entirely satisfactory, for self-criticism to be able to gain a foothold.

Of course there are, both in life and in literature, some very nice people who are simply satisfied with life, period. This is not a bad way to be. But that does not mean that it is optimal. The word "smug" probably would be too harsh for some of these cases. But the argument remains that it is not an ideal way to be, because it limits growth and improvement.

There also are cases that are not so attractive, and even less ideal. Everyone knows that someone who is always totally sure that everything that he or she does or feels is exemplary, without doubt, can be irritating. This form of complete happiness amounts to extreme smugness or complacency. That it is irritating is a causal feature that counts against it. The present argument suggests that, apart from its causal connections, it is in itself a defective state. Even apart from the causal connections, no one should want to be an extremely smug or complacent person. If this is so, then no one should want to be at the positive extreme of the happiness range.

The argument on this crucial point can be put as follows.

1. Complacency and limited openness to criticism are serious enough deficiencies that any mindset that includes them cannot be considered entirely satisfactory

2. Complete happiness entails complacency and limited openness to criticism

3. Therefore complete happiness cannot be desirable.

How can we decide whether (1) is correct? More generally, how can we decide what we should want, that is, what is really desirable in life? What we have to go on is mainly our sense of what it would be like. This sense can be the result of personal experience of various possibilities at least fleetingly, or empathetic observation of people who exemplify possibilities. Portrayals in the arts (although such sources cannot be taken uncritically) of what it would be like to have certain kinds of life also can play a part. Most of us have some sense of what it would be like to be an extremely smug or complacent person. My impression is that most people would consider it a defective state. We can embrace the appeal of a high degree of self-acceptance while realizing that to go higher still (to entire self-acceptance) would have significant negative features.

## Conclusion

Happiness surely would be, for most people, a major contributor to a very good life. The positive affect involved in having good moods much of the time becomes itself a reward. Further, as we have seen, one's relation to oneself has a special role in happiness. Clearly then happiness includes minimization of inner conflict, and normally that is an important good.

The value of happiness surely depends on the kind of life in which one is happy. Happiness in life as an idiot would not be considered highly desirable. Arguably something comparable can be said about happiness in a life that centers on causing suffering in others, or happiness in a life that is utterly trivial. Like most (perhaps all) values, that of happiness is contextual. What it is worth depends on the surrounding factors, including especially the kind of life that the happy person has.

It is often tempting to think very simply, and to regard a single factor as the key to everything. The limitations of happiness as a single-factor measure of quality of life can be seen when we consider the ideal of extreme happiness. Such a state would carry with it grave risks. It also would be undesirable in itself, including within itself smugness or complacency that no reasonable person should want to have.

Is there some positive message here about happiness? Much here is positive. Happiness depends greatly, as the psychologist Michael Argyle points out, on your general feeling about yourself and your life. It generally makes sense to want to be happy; happiness is nice. This points toward a concern with the general shape of your life, over and beyond particular details.

We often think of things or experiences that we want as crucial to happiness. The thought is "If I get that, then I will be happy." Sometimes such things will make a real long range difference to happiness; but very often the happiness instead will be *about* such-and-such, for a limited period after one gets it. The argument of this chapter suggests that any project of arriving at a long-term happiness that is worth something can start with an attempt to get a life about which you can reasonably be positive. To put happiness ahead of this is to put the cart before the horse.

# Myth Three

## THE GOOD LIFE REQUIRES REACHING A GOOD EQUILIBRIUM, A POINT AT WHICH THE IMPORTANT DIFFICULTIES ARE RESOLVED

Part of the allure of the ideal of complete happiness is that all problems would be resolved at that point. One could then, as it were, coast through life. The last chapter argued that complete happiness in fact would be extremely risky, and also, because of the constituent factors of smugness or complacency, would be unwholesome. The great attractiveness of the idea however is overdetermined. There is the appeal of total self-acceptance and of a reliable source of good moods. But there is also the appeal of being able, while still alive, to declare victory—once and for all—in the game of life.

This chapter will examine, and will attempt to diminish, the power of a comparable—but usually less extreme—vision of a good life. By "a good equilibrium" I mean a point at which one might think that life is much as it should be, and could assume (or hope) that it would continue like that indefinitely. A sense that reaching this is an important part of achieving a good life can be exceptionally deep-rooted. Let me confess that, despite everything that I have thought and am about to write, it has some hold over me. Part of its power is that many of us think of the future in terms of markers, points at which whatever is causing stress or worry or uncertainty will have receded. So I might think longingly, "In a couple of weeks, when such-and-such troublesome matters have been dealt with" or "When this book is finished." Often there are widely recognized markers for when Real Life is to begin. Familiar ones are "When I graduate," "When I am married," "When I get that job for which I have prepared."

There are long traditions, reflected in stories, plays, and now in movies, that involve the use of such markers. When Aristotle speaks of a narrative as having a beginning, a middle, and an end, he does not need to say what could constitute an end. The death of the protagonist counts as an end, in his culture and in ours (although perhaps not in traditional Tibetan culture, because of the importance given to how one maneuvers in the weeks after death).[1] A marriage counts as an end. This is a common end-point in fiction, plays, and movies; the universality of this may encourage the risky inclination to think of it as the point at which all significant problems have been solved. Finally, the victory or defeat of the protago-nist in some struggle or war will count as an end. This too can obscure the ways in which problems can persist, including those of keeping the peace, coming to terms with defeat and its aftermath, or of not becom-ing complacent and careless in victory.

The argument that follows, against the ideal of an equilibrium in life, will have two elements. First, it will explore the risks—things that can go badly wrong. Secondly, it will examine the constitutive impoverish-ment—the losses in life that are inherent in a life governed by the ideal.

## Some Risks of Looking Forward to an Equilibrium

Some obvious risks of the habit of looking forward to equilibrium points in life grow out of complacency, which includes being off-guard and not mindful when a looked-for equilibrium is reached. But there are others. The precise nature of the risks varies, depending on what the equilibrium point involves. We can begin by surveying the risks connected with the most common kinds of events that are thought of as equilibrium points.

One such point, often at or shortly after graduation, is getting a job. This is typically important in more ways than one. Usually it involves a new status as a fully "productive" member of society. Also, whatever is the character of the work will be likely to have major effects on the develop-ment of personality. The habits of mind of the work are almost certain to affect one's mindset in a wide range of situations. To start work as a chemist is to embark on a very different style of thinking from that involved in starting as a debt collector. The former would normally encourage a bent toward stability and reliable truths, and the latter might heighten any tendencies toward suspiciousness. A number of years of a

1. See *The Tibetan Book of the Dead*.

certain kind of work is likely, in various subtle ways, to transform one into a somewhat different kind of person.

This is worth considering. Also worth thinking about are all the parts of life that lie outside of work. Work will occupy nearly half a person's waking hours, and in some demanding professions perhaps more than half. But considerable time remains besides. The quality of what happens outside work can matter a great deal to the quality of life, more especially because—just as some income is "disposable" whereas other income is earmarked for fixed or inevitable expenses—time away from work typically is "disposable."

One trap lies in building up an increasingly sharp contrast between work and nonwork, so that they become extreme opposites. Work can lack independence and interest, and if so may be felt as demanding and imprisoning. The compensating thrust can be to make nonwork feel as independent and free as possible. If work involves a leaden discipline, nonwork can be entirely undisciplined, just sheer fun.

Much of this can be healthy, normal, and inevitable. But the life to which it can lead may not turn out to be very satisfactory. The vulnerability of fun to the hedonic treadmill should be clear from the first chapter. The alternative to the extreme of fun-seeking—use of some nonwork time to develop skills and pursue skilled activities—is much more likely to lead to long-term satisfaction.

Consider also a banal point. Increasingly, a first job is almost always not the last job. Regarding getting the first job as an equilibrium point in life makes it easy to overlook preparation for what might be the second or third job. In particular, a narrow focus on what is required for that first job can put someone at a serious disadvantage in being ready for anything later that is different.

All these things need attention in crafting a good life once the marker point of getting the job has been passed. Someone who has fixated on that as an equilibrium point risks thinking "Now that that is over, I can really live." Sometimes this is a coded way of accepting a lazy organization of life, which can lead to missed opportunities and to habits of mind that flow away from a really satisfying existence.

The risks of a narrow focus on marriage as an equilibrium point are not entirely the same, but there are one or two similarities. Marriage is a primary relationship that, once entered upon, turns out not to be a current that sweeps one along. There continue to be a huge number of choices within the relationship and ample room to maneuver in ways that can affect the strength of the marriage and the quality of life for both parties. A great deal of living takes place outside of the primary relationship that needs thinking about. As everyone knows (but people sometimes forget), a badly managed outer life can affect the quality of the shared life. Again, the idea that an equilibrium point has been reached can work against mindfulness that is useful and necessary.

Career successes, especially when they involve status and security, also can seem like equilibrium points. Examples would be making partner in a law firm, or gaining academic tenure. By now it should be obvious what are some of the risks. They include not thinking reflectively about surrounding factors that make a great difference to the quality of life.

Some specific risks lie in any moment at which someone can, so to speak, declare success in life. One is that the hitherto extremely industrious person can become a bit of a slacker—secure at last—or at the least coast through the rest of her or his life. A related risk is that of missed opportunity. In most forms of work, even work conducted independently, there is some need to please others, to do what they want, and to meet their standards. Typically this never entirely goes away, but career successes that involve security do diminish the pressure to please others and meet their standards. In professions that are somewhat conformist, this can be a golden opportunity to pursue projects that are highly promising but also risky, or generally to have a more independent style of work.

Clearly risks of a different sort lie in what I have just suggested. The highly independent kind of work may not turn out to be good. Nevertheless, sometimes there is a real possibility of original and interesting work, which could be quite satisfying for the now-secure person who accomplishes it. It would be a pity if the newly secure professional missed her or his opportunity for this. To regard the career success simply as an equilibrium point, focusing on the sense that there is no longer anything to worry about, can subtly discourage what could be both important and gratifying.

A final widely recognized equilibrium point (if one leaves aside death) is retirement. This is an event that often has two contrasting aspects. The first is the sense of unlimited freedom. One can do anything one wants with one's time. The other is the sense of emptiness. There may be nothing one has to do with one's time. In addition, the feeling of something further to look forward to (another equilibrium point further down the line) may be lacking.

The opportunities to do something interesting with the freedom and the empty time can vary, of course, from person to person. The greatest temptation of this particular equilibrium point in life often includes the following. The retiree, now excused from gainful work (and presumably also no longer raising a family), can extend this sense of being excused and freed to all of life. This sometimes can have attractive results, as the newly excused give themselves permission to do things (such as starting conversations with strangers, or voicing opinions that they had been shy about articulating) which can contribute to the liveliness of life. The risk is that this general sense of being excused can lead, even if skilled activities on a regular basis are possible, to a failure to organize any such pattern of activities. In the worst case, the sense that an equilibrium point has been reached can undermine habits of self-discipline at just the moment at which self-discipline becomes most crucial to the quality of life.

## Generic Risks of the Mindset of Looking Forward to an Equilibrium

Thus far we have looked mainly at risks that are specific to each of the common equilibrium points. Some risks do recur. A more careless attitude toward the quality of life is a recurrent risk of thinking one has just reached an equilibrium point. There exist other generic risks of looking toward any moment in life as an equilibrium point. These include a lack of long-term thinking past the equilibrium.

This risk is obvious, but also is easily overlooked. It is over-determined. For one thing, in the last few decades (at least in America), there has been a noticeable decline in long-term thinking, sometimes in personal life but most prominently among business leaders, politicians, and policy makers. This is heightened by the fact that so many decision-making positions are transitory. The person making decisions can hope that things will go well while she or he is in charge. Often the chances of this can be improved by postponing difficulties and seizing immediate advantages, with the almost inevitable result that in the longer run things may go very badly indeed. The mentality of seizing immediate advantages and postponing problems (which then may well grow larger) naturally spreads from business and politics to ordinary life.

Even apart from this, at some moments it is especially tempting to focus on the short run, especially when there is the prospect of great short-term benefits. These moments include most of the equilibrium points in people's lives. The mood of the moment affects one's view of everything. If the equilibrium point is of a positive sort, then there will be a period (usually somewhat brief) before the hedonic treadmill begins to operate. It will seem that life has been transformed forever, a very relaxing supposition.

Why, some readers may wonder, am I going on about the importance of long-term thinking in personal life? There are three main reasons. First, consider elementary prudence. Organizing oneself for the future does not mean that one can chart the future with great confidence. In fact it requires a degree of preparation for contingencies, even remote contingencies. Positive opportunities do not, by and large, happen out of the blue. Typically they happen to people who have positioned themselves appropriately, and in that sense are ready for them. Negative events—threats or deprivations—also do not always happen out of the blue; sometimes there are ways of minimizing their likelihood, or lessening their likely impact if they occur. Safeguards can be put in place. The great Chinese philosopher Mencius, who lived in the fourth century BCE, remarks that a pattern of "perennial worries" can create a life in which there are no "unexpected vexations," by which I think he means that the wariness involved in moderate worry protects one from real upset or anxiety.[2] This idea suggests that problems are best dealt with when they are still small.

A second reason for the importance of long-term thinking is that so many of the most valuable things in life are built incrementally. Think of the sequences of skilled activities that Csikszentmihalyi's subjects considered to be peak experiences. Their skills typically were not entirely innate (although they may well have built on native aptitude), nor were they typically acquired to their full degree in a very short period of time. A pattern of skill acquisition precedes the pattern of fulfilling experiences.

---

2. *Mencius,* trans. D. C. Lau (Harmondsworth: Penguin, 1970), Book IV Part B, 134. A reader may wonder how this squares with the observation in Chapter 1 that when people lose themselves in sequences of skilled activity there typically is no anxious concern for the outcome (although there can have been thoughts about how things might go). This is discussed in the Appendix, Number 10.

Besides skills themselves, one has to acquire an organization of life that allows time and energy for using these skills. Again this is unlikely to be the result of an instant transformation. The stage setting as well as the skills would normally be within the province of long-term thinking, which thus contributes to building a deeply satisfying life.

Another factor alluded to in the first chapter that may be exempt from the hedonic treadmill is the satisfactions within personal relations. The ones that seem most likely to be exempt are those that represent a well-established pattern of mutual caring, in contrast to shallow and possibly transitory personal relations of a more directly pleasure-seeking sort. Common experience tells us that the first kind of personal relationship, which can provide lasting satisfaction, typically develops in an incremental fashion. Even if there are glances across a room as a starting point, these relations can offer much over a significant period of time only with a sustained emotional investment on both sides. Perhaps the previous sentence should read "on all sides," because of course not all deeply satisfying personal relations are those of couples. There are the meaningful relations within a family, a neighborhood, or a community. People who lack all of these, whatever their casual pleasures may be, are pitiable.

A third reason for the importance of long-term thinking is that much of what will seem meaningful in a person's life connects different moments in time. The sense that one's life has meaning is a source of deep satisfaction, and its absence can be a source of real dissatisfaction. The sense of meaning, though, is not far removed from the sense of structure.

Much of this structure can be provided by purposes, which to some degree then perhaps are fulfilled. Even if they are not fulfilled, if there was a good and wholehearted effort this can seem important and really valuable. A book by Ivan Morris, *The Nobility of Failure,* examines this idea in traditional Japanese culture.

Other elements also can help to integrate a life. Habits of mind, interests, and long-term relationships can provide binding elements. Continuity of habitual ways of doing things, which is part of what we think of loosely and unphilosophically as being the same person, also can play a major part. It should be emphasized that the notion that an integrated life can be more meaningful does not imply that people do not, or should not, ever change. It certainly does count against a life filled with abrupt and spasmodic change, although in some cases this might provide an odd sort of stylistic continuity.

A normal, intelligent person may well change some habits of mind, many interests, and perhaps some long-term relationships in the course of an integrated and meaningful life. Even where there is change, there can be underlying connections between what was before and what came after. By and large, change that makes sense against the background of earlier interests and purposes is compatible with an integrated life, and change that seems more random usually is not. Because of persistent themes, or similarities of purpose in various episodes, a life that is full of variety can still seem "all of a piece." An integrated life need not be a monotonous one.

Much of the preceding might remind a few readers of a phrase some-times used by philosophers, speaking of a person's "plan of life." Let me distance myself from this in one respect. It is usually absurd to have a plan of life, if that is held to entail a firm sense of the major things that will (or should) occur in that life. The future is rarely that predictable, and anyway we should be free to change our minds about some of our goals or inter-ests. If "plan of life" means a blueprint, then having one often would carry its own risks.

What if a plan of life means an organization, along the lines of cur-rent purposes and interests, of a possible course of life that looks like it would be satisfying—if the plan allows latitude, and gives room for changes of direction? Something like that can be recommended. It cer-tainly is superior to any rigid plan on one hand and also to sheer thoughtlessness on the other. It should be said though that sheer thoughtlessness does not always doom someone to a meaningless life or one that is lacking in structure. Sometimes structure and meaning can develop as things go on. Usually prior long-term thinking will have improved the odds for this to happen effectively, but improvisation does seem to work for some people.

To sum up this section: the mindset of looking forward to equilibri-um points in life undermines long-term thinking. But long-term think-ing contributes to prudent organization, including preparation for con-tingencies that could change the quality of life. Long-term thinking also contributes to the incremental process of building up gratifying person-al relationships and patterns of skilled activities. Finally, long-term think-ing usually (although not always) does better than sheer improvisation over time in creating an integrated structure that will make a life seem more meaningful.

## *Processes vs. Goalposts*

Beyond all this, the mindset of looking forward to equilibrium points encourages the tendency to view the values of life in terms of goalposts rather than processes. To be governed by this mindset is to miss a great deal. The focus on goals engenders inattention to what does not promote or obstruct their realization.

This can best be understood if we explore the contrast of the prospective (forward-looking) view of what is important in life with the retrospective view. Neither has a monopoly on sanity, but there are interesting differences. Retrospective views sometimes light up values that were largely ignored (and thus diminished) at the time.

In the first chapter it was mentioned that we human beings appear to be wired with a strong desire-pleasure nexus guiding our lives. This may have been very useful for cavemen and cavewomen, pursuing the primitive goals of survival and reproduction. But the advantages of the power of the desire-pleasure nexus, like the advantages that the sinus formerly offered our ancestors moving on all fours, may have dwindled under changed conditions. Much of classical Indian philosophy centers on arguments that these features of normal human nature are now a psychological trap, and that eliminating their influence over us would be worth the hard work required.

For most of us, the prospective view of what is important in human life centers on the things that we really desire. Chief among these are things that mark a change of status (e.g., a position that has greater rewards or higher prestige). Once we have something of this sort, we think, life will be finer and better. This is what I mean by goalposts.

When people look back at portions of their lives, sometimes the goalposts do have a major role, especially if reaching them represented a real achievement. This is a kind of satisfaction, linked to sense of self, that typically never goes away. Very often however, people also look back fondly to the period of working and hoping that led to the achievement. They feel that they were doing something meaningful, and were "really alive."

One odd example of the disjunct between the prospective and the retrospective views concerns military service. A surprising number of people appear to look back fondly on a set of experiences that at the time clearly were wretched. In this case, especially when the service was in the peacetime army, there is little suggestion that the activities were especially meaningful. The effort of getting through them may have seemed meaningful, but perhaps a larger factor in the nostalgia is the camaraderie among people living in close quarters and dealing with the same irritations and problems. For some of them, this may have been the closest network of human relations they would ever experience. At the time those experiences would simply be regarded as wretched, because the focus would be so strongly on the irritations and the problems. But in retrospect, a very positive element amidst the wretchedness comes into clearer view.

Ironically it seems that the more difficult something was—the more dissatisfactions there were along the way—the more fondly people look back on it. Having overcome, or least dealt with, the difficulties and the dissatisfactions comes to seem intensely meaningful. This is especially true of struggles to achieve something that did not come at all easily.

The contrast, in short, lies between how it seemed at the time, an image dominated by the goalposts and the hope and anxiety directed toward them (or, in the case of the military service, by dissatisfactions and irritations), and how it seems in retrospect. Does one of these views have better claims to be taken seriously than the other? Which is more important?

Questions of this sort recur in relation to values. There are some respects in which we know that retrospective views are highly flawed. The major example in recent psychological literature, reported in the first chapter, concerns memories of an extended painful experience. Typically, how bad people remember that time to have been is determined by how bad it was at its peak and at the very end. Duration, which one might think matters, drops out.[3]

In the light of this, it is very tempting to discount any retrospective evaluations, whatever their objects. Some retrospective evaluations are clearly very flawed. There are reasons, though, for thinking that the positive retrospective evaluations of a period of struggle and difficulty that led to an achievement are not flawed and should be taken seriously.

Here is one reason. The view that someone at the time would have had of the process of working toward goals, with all of its difficulties and dissatisfactions, would depend greatly on how detached that person is. A

3. See Daniel Kahneman, "Objective Happiness," in Kahneman et al., eds., *Well-Being* (New York: Russell Sage, 1999), 3–25.

judgment of value is likely to inspire more confidence if it is grounded in a full and clear sense of what is evaluated. But someone who is highly concerned with a set of goals, and who is not at all detached, is unlikely to have a full and clear sense at the moment of what is going on in her or his life.

This is because an anxiousness-laden focus on goals creates a kind of tunnel vision. One sees forward to the attainment, or nonattainment, of goals; this preoccupation gets in the way of appreciating anything that is to the side of this project. It also gets in the way of any appreciation of the texture and quality of the very process of trying to attain goals.

Phenomena of this sort are familiar to many people. In a sequence of skilled activities, say in music-making or in athletics, someone who is very worried about results is much more likely not to notice things happening off to the side (or that are peripheral to the main activity) than someone who is carried along by the activity and not at all anxious. Paradoxically, more thorough involvement often makes possible greater alertness.

A not entirely dissimilar point applies to the irritation-laden experience that many people report as a focus of military service. There too lies a narrowing of focus. The irritation-sensitive mindset highlights negative features of the overall experience, which we can usually assume were entirely genuine. But the positive features of what was involved in processes of coping, and also in the camaraderie engendered, receded into the shadows at the time. Later they will be much more appreciated.

Let us concentrate on the temporal displacement involved in focusing on goals. Much of this will be discussed shortly under the heading of living in the future. Of course no one can literally live in the future. But if a person's emotional focus is localized in the future in a very pronounced way, then the wished for (or dreaded) future will seem like where one belongs, and much of the present will be very shadowy indeed.

Later on, a person can remember things that barely registered at the time. Much anxiety will be removed from this retrospective view, because after all one knows how things turned out. Often it is plausible to suppose that the calmer view, which is the retrospective one rather than the view at the time, is more objective.

Goalposts will not entirely disappear from this calmer, retrospective view. After all, what is viewed was in large part an attempt to gain (or to avoid, or to get through) such and such. But there will be a larger place for the process of trying to gain, avoid, or get through such and such. The series of actions that lead (or fail to lead) to the goal will come to seem more important, and no longer merely a means to an end. There will be room now for appreciation of the texture of the endeavor, its meaningful properties, the way in which one was really engaged in activities, the comradeship with others in similar situations, etc.

In the end, one of two things will likely be the case. One is that the goal that was so much cared about will seem, given hindsight, not to have mattered so much to the quality of life. The other is that the goal indeed mattered, and mattered especially because it made possible further processes of life that are valuable (involving personal relationships, or skilled activities of various sorts). Often the most genuinely important goals are the ones that create abilities and opportunities of these sorts. The hope then must be that these further processes of life are appreciated as they occur, instead of their appreciation being postponed to some later date.

## Living in the Present vs. Living in the Future

There is a running argument in much Asian philosophy—especially that associated with Chinese Daoism or the Chan Buddhism in China that in Japan became Zen—that the temporal displacement involved in any anxiety-laden focus on goals impairs the quality of life. In the view of these philosophies, much of the value in our lives is determined by the harmonious emotional quality of our responses to what is happening.

The nature of this argument deserves careful attention, especially because it looks grounded in considerable experience both of unsatisfactory patterns of human life and of alternatives, which in the long run are extremely satisfying. Some common misunderstandings first need to be resolved.

Many of us in the West can come to feel that prevailing patterns of life are too tense. What might seem appealing, then, is the extreme opposite of tension: an easygoing mindless kind of relaxation. At first glance it might seem as if this is what is promised by philosophies like those of Daoism or Zen.

This is a mistake. Zen practitioners report, first of all, that the training required to achieve the recommended attitudes is not at all relaxed. Real effort, which includes dissatisfaction with the unsatisfactory self with which one began, is a major part of what goes on. It is stressful work.

Even when the recommended attitudes are achieved, they would be better described as "poised" than as relaxed. They certainly are not mindless. Poem 15 (in the traditional numbering) in the *Daodejing* describes the masters of old as

> Poised, like one who must ford a stream in winter.
>
> Cautious, like one who fears his neighbors on every side.[4]

Only a fool ignores danger or difficulties, and recommended attitudes of Daoism and Zen do not include being a fool. They also do not include being worked up, or nervous, or agitated about dangers and difficulties. A calm, poised person can make note of dangers and do what is safe and appropriate in a calm, collected way. This eschews any emotion-laden focus on the future, but it does not involve casting a blind eye on possible developments.

There is a very nice portrayal of enlightened coping in another Daoist work, the *Chuang-Tzu* (sometimes rendered as *Zhuangzi*). The enlightened character is Cook Ting, who is especially skilled at cutting up oxen.[5] There is objective evidence of his skill: "A good cook normally changes his chopper once a year, because he hacks." Cook Ting has had his chopper for nineteen years, and the blade is still fresh, because of his skill in sliding through the tiny openings in the meat. It is as if Ting is guided in this by an inner spirit. "Whenever I come to something intricate, I see where it will be hard to handle and cautiously prepare myself, my gaze settles on it, action slows down for it." And then Cook Ting gives the right stroke and feels proud and happy.

There is no mindlessness or carelessness here. It should be emphasized that the attentiveness that Cook Ting gives to difficulties involves extraordinary clarity. It is simply true that sometimes one needs unusual clarity in order to deal with things. This is one of the reasons why strong emotions are often counterproductive. They tend to narrow a person's focus, so that less detail is taken in. Therefore anxiousness about the future not only detracts from the quality of present experience; it also impairs performance. An enlightened person would eliminate these strong emotions

---

4. *Daodejing* of Lao Tzi, trans. Philip J. Ivanhoe (Indianapolis: Hackett Publishing Co., 2002), 15.

5. *Chuang-Tzu: The Inner Chapters,* trans. A. C. Graham (Indianapolis: Hackett Publishing Co., 2001), pp. 63–4.

and the tight focus on goals and dangers, and because of this would perform better.

Zen literature especially emphasizes the fuller, more detailed view of
the world that becomes possible when one develops the requisite poise.
This includes an extreme awareness of detail. This is illustrated by a
story about someone who has qualified as a Zen teacher and visits his
old master.[6] It was a rainy day, and the teacher, having worn wooden
clogs and carried an umbrella, left them in the vestibule. When he
enters, his old master asks him whether he had left his umbrella to the
left or the right of the clogs. The newly qualified teacher realizes with
a shock that he does not know. So he goes back for six more years as a
pupil.

By itself, the awareness of detail can be impressive. (It also can make a
difference in building cars and electronic equipment, but that is another
matter.) But is awareness of detail important to the quality of life? The
Zen answer is built around an aesthetic claim that the world—anything
in the world—is beautiful, if seen with properly appreciative eyes. Thus a
major reward of the difficult Zen training, it is claimed, is an ongoing
experience of beauty. The world and one's life in the world can be
savored.

For many of us life is not like this. Perhaps, as the *New Testament* puts
it, for us the salt has lost its savor? (Should we be more like "the lilies of
the field"?) Indeed, religious and philosophical issues about the quality of
life run close together at points like this. Let us stick to the philosophical,
and investigate how the thesis of the beauty of the world could be argued
for and defended.

The most obvious objection is that there are so many ugly things in
the world. Not only does this suggest that the world is, at best, beautiful
only in parts. It also suggests that the attention to detail that Daoism and
Zen are designed to promote could lead to greater awareness of, and
exposure to, real ugliness.

It seems to me that a Daoist or a Zen Buddhist could concede that
there are things in the world (such as sunsets and majestic mountains) that
lend themselves to experiences of great beauty. These things are easy to
see as beautiful. When we single them out as beautiful, that is what we

---

6. *Zen Flesh, Zen Bones,* eds. P. Reps and N. Senzaki (Boston: Tuttle, 1985), story number 35 of 101 Zen Stories, 53–4.

mean. There are other things that people normally cannot see as beautiful; they are normally seen as ugly. This is what we mean by speaking of ugly things.

The claim though is that a visually gifted person, someone with a transforming vision that included great attention to detail, could have a beautiful experience of anything. Great artists provide examples of this. A Rembrandt painting in the Louvre portrays a side of beef, something not normally thought to be lovely, that is beautiful. Presumably Rembrandt could have produced a beautiful painting of a pile of garbage. There is a story about the Italian renaissance painter Luca Signorelli along similar but more poignant lines. Signorelli's much beloved son was killed. In his grief, the painter asked that the corpse be brought to him. "Even as he grieved, Luca had the body stripped, and with the greatest constancy of heart, without crying or shedding a tear, he drew his portrait."[7]

The argument that anything can be seen as beautiful is not entirely abstract, but rather is meant to rest on psychological claims about human beings in general. Two claims stand out. One is that the normal psychological state for a human being involves a mind that is cluttered and confused. The other is that, if a process of emptying and calming the mind is pursued, the resulting clarity will result in repeated experiences of great beauty.

The first claim may seem more obviously plausible than the second. Think about what a mind—reader would access in the minds of almost all of us. Stray thoughts pop into the mind. The mind wanders, now being reminded of such and such, now suddenly attentive to something else, but only for a minute or so. The effect would be much more like hearing an orchestra tune up than hearing it play a recognizable composition.

Because there is so much going on, and we are preoccupied, our perceptions tend to be schematic. We notice if there is a tree, a car, or a person we know near us. But the colors and shapes of the leaves on the tree, or the clouds in the sky above it, or details in the appearance of the car or of our acquaintance simply may not register in any clear way. This has practical advantages in speeding us on our way. But it

---

7. Giorgio Vasari, *The Lives of the Artists,* trans. Julia Conaway Bondonella and Peter Bondonella (Oxford: Oxford World Classics, 1998), 271.

represents an impoverished world of experience for almost all of our waking lives.

It may sound odd to speak of emptying the mind as a way that our experience can be made richer, especially when the result is said to promise great awareness of detail. What is supposed to be emptied from the mind? The Way, according to Poem No. 48 (in the traditional numbering) of the *Daodejing,* is to be gained by daily loss.[8] What is supposed to be lost?

Part of the answer rests in the confused babel of stray thoughts that pop into and out of the mind, often leading nowhere. Much of the answer has to do with the emotions. The *Chuang-Tzu* speaks of fasting of the mind/heart. A large part of this involves not having strong emotions, especially those of concern for the future. Fasting is not the same as starvation. The enlightened Daoist or Zen Buddhist is assumed to have some emotions, including especially emotions of spontaneous delight in things, and also mild preferences of various sorts (e.g., a mild preference not to be eaten by a tiger, which can result in careful behavior while in areas where tigers live). But the strong, urgent emotions of fear and desire will be absent. This will have the effect of emptying out the matrix of thoughts of how really nice or awful such-and-such would be, and the random hopeful or fearful thoughts that collect around these.

In the abstract, it would seem equally possible that an emptied-out mind would have a positive outlook and experiences or a negative outlook and experiences. Daoist and Zen testimonials, along with observation of people who seem to have met their standards for

---

8. *Daodejing,* trans. Blakney, 101. There is a complex thought here. Another element is very well presented in Philip J. Ivanhoe's translation of Poem Number 48.

"In the pursuit of the Way, one does less every day.

One does less and less until one does nothing;

One does nothing yet nothing is left undone."

The poem plays on two senses of what it is to be "doing something." One describes an overt push or pull at the world. Consider that when someone asks you what you are doing, and you reply "nothing," that cannot be literally true. Quiet friendly time spent with people can be "doing nothing," but can build friendships, change moods, etc. The Daoist view is that pushing or pulling at the world is often (perhaps always) counterproductive, but that a lot can be accomplished by doing what looks like nothing.

enlightenment, support the positive story. Underneath the confused thoughts and emotional surges that dominate the lives of most of us, it is claimed, lies something that (when calm and peaceful) will have remarkably positive experiences—and also positive attitudes towards others. This amounts to an optimistic view of human nature as it might be: in other words, of the potential human nature that underlies what we are actually like. Normal human nature—what virtually all of us are like—on the other hand involves mistakes, confusion, and needless anxiety. The prescription is a kind of psychological training, which is demanding and requires one's full attention, which is designed gradually to transform a person's nature, until it approximates the highly advantageous nature that is latent in all of us.

The recommendation in short is drastic, and would have the effect of taking someone out of what most of us would consider to be the normal patterns of human life. It is always possible to judge that perhaps the cure would be worse than the disease. Let me put this thought to the side. (For one thing I am in no position to evaluate it.) Instead, let me suggest that a wider range of options exists than might at first appear, for someone who accepts the Daoist and Zen Buddhist diagnosis of endemic problems in "normal" human life but is wary of the recommended course of treatment.

This is because "fasting of the heart" is a matter of degree. It cannot too strongly be emphasized, to begin with, that the Daoist and Zen Buddhist recommendations do not include a total removal of emotions. In the end there are supposed to be many spontaneous pleasures (of the sort not preceded by desire, great hope, or anxiety) and many little joys. And there can be mild aversions, typified by the mild preference not to be eaten by a tiger. Emotions in short will be lower-key than is usually the case. They also will be on the whole oriented to what is going on, although there can be the mild prospective emotions involved in avoiding tigers and, in Cook Ting's case, preferring to make an exceptionally clean cut in the meat.

Without giving up most of what generally is considered normal life, any one of us could diminish the strength of emotions, especially those that involve desire or anxiety for the future. The result of a degree of movement in this direction would almost certainly not involve the joys claimed for enlightened Daoists or Zen Buddhists. But it might well involve more spontaneous pleasures, a bit more joy, and a greater aware-ness and savoring of the surroundings of everyday life.

A delicate balancing act would be required in this (as well as in the full-strength Daoist or Zen recommendation). First, it could arguably be advantageous to have milder emotions—but not advantageous, on the other hand, to be affectless. Secondly, one would want especially to diminish the power of prospective emotions without entirely eliminating attentiveness to what concerns the future.

One can only conjecture how many people walk in front of cars every year because their minds are on desires or anxieties. It is surely not a large number, but it might not be negligible. Regardless of what it is, one would not want people walking in front of cars because of newly acquired entire indifference to the future. Any recommended solution has to be an attitude nicely balanced somewhere in the middle.

## Conclusion

The view of life that keeps looking forward to a stable equilibrium, at which one feels that real life will begin, has many disadvantages. The focus on what is hoped for lessens attention to other factors that may lead to great satisfaction or dissatisfaction later. When the stable equilibrium is thought not to be far ahead, this view of life in general discourages long-term thinking of the sort that is conducive to prudence and also to the integration of a person's life.

Perhaps the greatest disadvantage inherent in this view of life—because the focus is on the future rather than the present—is that it postpones the savoring of life. Many people do gain a sense that some savoring of ongoing experiences and the processes of life enhances the quality of life. Narrowing one's attention by concentrating on future goals slights many of the factors that retrospectively could be seen to be important to the quality of life. Further, because this outlook is habit-forming, it postpones the savoring of much of life not only once or twice, but indefinitely.

A positive message is that it is possible to work towards goals and yet savor values of the present. The trick is to organize activities around a focused preference for success, but at the same time to be detached enough to permit a broad awareness of the surrounding qualities of life. This can be viewed as part of a broader point. Much that is important in life involves not only working on the world, but also working on ourselves.

# Myth Four

## REASON RATHER THAN EMOTIONS WOULD BE THE BEST INDICATOR OF WHAT WOULD BE A GOOD LIFE

We all need to be rational, especially when something important is at stake. What could be more personally important than whether we have good lives? Therefore it may seem obvious that reason tells us what would count as a good life.

This is at best a one-sided view, and in many cases a glaring mistake. If a wide range of people make this mistake, most of them not philosophers, much of the fault lies in loose talk by philosophers. Often in philosophical discourse words like "rational" and "reasonable" are used as terms of convenience. They are used to praise what a philosopher wants other people to agree with. Such talk typically is not accompanied by any careful analysis of just what the philosopher might mean by "rational" and "reasonable." A corrective is to look at the variety of meanings that these words can have.

## Reason, Rationality, and Reasonableness

What is it to be rational? The word typically refers to a cluster of desirable properties of thought. Four of these stand out.

First there is a property that connects being rational with a narrow sense of "reason," one that is at the core of the traditional meaning. In this sense, reason is the process of making sound logical inferences. Traditionally, these are either deductive or inductive. Deductive inferences yield conclusions that were implicit in their starting points. For example, if Socrates is a man and all men are mortal, then deductive reason tells us that Socrates is mortal. Inductive inferences yield the likelihood that, barring intervening factors, new experiences will follow the established pattern of what we have already experienced. Thus inductive reason tells us that, barring intervening factors, the sun very likely will rise tomorrow and the next crow we see very likely will be black.

There is a broader sense of "reason," and of "rational," that concerns the ability to pick out good reasons (and reject bad ones) in support of a conclusion, and to be governed by them. Reason in this sense tells us that the fact that Mary had a good chance to steal a lot of money (and almost certainly wouldn't have been detected)—and that she rejected this opportunity—is good evidence that she has some significant degree of virtue. Reason in the broader sense also tells us that the fact that someone smiles a lot and has a firm handshake is not good evidence for a conclusion of that sort.

If the core of "reason" is logical competence, then what I have called "reason" in a broader sense counts as reason only in a marginal way. Really it is a matter of intelligent thinking. What enables an intelligent person to realize that smiling and having a firm handshake do not amount to evidence of virtue is not primarily a logical inference. Rather it is some minimal experience of life, along with attentiveness and ability to retain what has been experienced.

You could call this "rational," but you equally well could call it "savvy." The one link with reason in the narrow sense is that there will be an awareness that possible inductive inferences fail. There will have been no pattern of people who smile and have firm handshakes overwhelmingly being virtuous. Hence any inductive inference that points in that direction can't get off the ground.

A third sense of "rational" has an even slighter connection with the core meaning of "reason" than the preceding one. Some (although by no means all) philosophers and economists have a taste for simple models of what matters in life, which can yield seemingly simple ways of making decisions. An especially beguiling one treats a single factor—say, how much money a person can manage to have—as decisive in determining the choices of what they call a "rational agent." A "rational" agent then (in this view) is one who does what leads to having the most possible money.

Virtually everyone would like to have more money, and there is no compelling reason why it should be disdained. But any reader should by now have a sharpened sense that there are many things besides money that are important to the quality of a person's life. If a simple model obscures this, this is a good reason for trying to think in a more complicated way.

Finally a sense of being rational comes into play when someone is governed by strong emotions, or by some fixed idea, which would not withstand reflective scrutiny. We say, "Be rational." If strong emotions are the problem, this is a way of saying, "Calm down and take a broader view." If the problem is a fixed idea, then it is a way of saying, "You should reconsider, and take seriously reasons that point in a different direction."

Note that strong emotions are not always inappropriate. To be really, really angry with someone who has been cruel or nasty may be quite justified. However a strong emotion that is justified may be, all the same, counterproductive in terms of correcting a bad situation. We may be more effective in doing something about it after we have calmed down.

One of the reasons why strong emotions often interfere with effective action is as follows. Often someone in the grip of the emotions will experience a drastically reduced focus, not taking in peripheral factors that are highly relevant to any effective action. A calmer person pursuing the same goals will be more likely to focus on the entire situation, and to adjust strategy accordingly.

Often the goals themselves need to be adjusted. Indeed strong emotions (which include intense anger, hatred, jealousy, loathing, and desire) may be, as a class, more prone to be misleading—either about what we are reacting to, or about what needs to be done—than milder emotions. So many of our strong emotions appear to be wired into us in a primal way and represent crude mechanisms of immediate response. Some of these would have been better adapted to the needs of survival in a savage society than to the demands of civilized life.

All of this is worth bearing in mind in that many of the classic criticisms of emotion apply to strong emotions but not to mild ones. Examples of emotions that are typically mild include delight, distaste, admiration, compassion, and appreciation. The critiques of emotion in ancient Greek, Indian, and Chinese philosophy by and large have to be read as applying to strong emotions and not to mild ones. Certainly no philosopher has ever held that we should be affectless.

The case against strong emotions—even justified ones (such as intense anger against evil)—has a number of elements. First (as already noted), because they typically narrow our focus and limit our awareness of detail and of the range of possibilities, they are counterproductive. Milder forms of the same kind of response would lead to more effective action. A more icy and low-key antipathy might in the long run be more successful.

Secondly, emotions can represent habits of mind just as much as do ordinary ideas. Strong emotions can come to us in a variety of ways, with a variety of objects. If you allow yourself to be in the grip of strong emotions, this risks a pattern of being jerked around by a series of strong emotions, being in love with love or in hate with hate.

Thirdly, ancient philosophers who cautioned against strong emotions all held that eliminating them would make room for milder emotions that would contribute much more to the quality of life. There certainly is no consensus, even within Indian philosophy or within Greek or Chinese philosophy, as to what the important milder emotions would be. But joy of an ongoing sort is presented in more than one philosophy as a reward of clearing one's mind of emotional disturbances. In the Chinese Daoist account, clearing the mind makes possible a playful and joyful spontaneity. A mild but steady compassion would be on Buddha's list. Plato and the Confucian philosophers hold that a disciplined and well-ordered mind would feature a psychic harmony, which would include an agreeable positive sense of the workings of one's own mind. As Chapter 2 pointed out, such an agreeable sense would contribute to a crucial element of happiness in the view of contemporary psychologists such as Michael Argyle.

To lose all emotions would point in the direction of an affectless, apathetic state, which is hardly appealing. Both in ordinary speech and in philosophy and psychology, "Don't be emotional about this" does not mean "Do not have any emotions whatsoever." Rather it expresses a caution about strong emotions, especially when they constrict thought processes or cause you to have fixed ideas. "Be rational" has much the same force, often with added emphasis on the suggestion that further thought might be desirable. One of the problems with strong emotions is that they often capture, and effectively end, thought processes on a given subject. Often second or third thoughts might help someone toward a more intelligent view (and toward a more intelligent emotional response).

"Be reasonable" often has much the force of "Be rational." Additionally, though, the word "reasonable" has features that make it almost irresistible to someone who is conducting an informal argument. In many contexts, "reasonable" means something very like "OK" or "This is what an intelligent person would agree with, don't you think?" Because of this, it is an especially appealing word for writers of philosophy to use. I must admit that it makes an appearance in various places in this book in that role.

The important point for this chapter is that the sense of "reasonable" under discussion has hardly any connection with the core sense of "reason." One factor that makes philosophers very often fall back on a vague sense of "reasonable" is that, with very few exceptions (the seventeenth-century Dutch philosopher Baruch [or Benedictus] Spinoza being the most prominent), philosophical arguments very rarely take the form of deductive logic. Needless to say, forms of inductive logic have been even more uncommon.

Philosophers typically do have arguments, but these rarely have the force of deductive or inductive inferences. Consequently the philosopher rarely can say, "You must believe my conclusion, if you have accepted the starting points of the argument," or even, "This argument makes the conclusion highly probable." Good arguments can provide real support to their conclusions. But in philosophy (as in politics, the law, and many other areas) the support is of a moderate sort that is hard to talk about. "Reasonable" then becomes a very convenient word. Usually it claims that what is said is not just a casual opinion but has been thought out, and that genuine reasons of some strength have been (or could be) given for it.

Yet another use of "reasonable" connects with the social dimensions of intelligence. Usually it is more intelligent to listen to other people and to take account of their views than to ignore them and complete all reflection within the circuit of one's own thoughts. There may be occasions when the people around you are very benighted, or so thoroughly out of sympathy with the main lines of your thought that fruitful exchange of ideas is clearly impossible. This is uncommon, and by and large we can learn something from others, even when in the end we need not accept most of what we are being told. There are real risks, on the other hand, in remaining confined within the circuit of one's own thoughts. Even an intelligent person can miss something, and even an intelligent view can be improved by details and nuances inspired by what others say.

It is also good for personal relations to listen to others and give some weight to their interests, in most situations. There can be exceptions, especially when something serious is involved and some of the other people at hand are willing to support evil. Someone determined to save innocent people from being killed probably should not listen to cowardly neighbors, although even here judgment is required; sometimes a degree of accommodation with the cowardly neighbors might increase the chances of success.

In most of ordinary life, though, when the stakes are not hugely high and the alternatives not dramatically opposed, it is simply intelligent to engage in some give-and-take discussion with the people at hand. That this can contribute to good personal relations has already been noted. This connects with a point that may at first seem counterintuitive: it can be dangerous to be entirely in the right on an issue in which not much is at stake. The sense of being in the right can make it too tempting to strain your connections seriously. The Confucian philosopher Mencius warns against "trying to dominate (people) through goodness."[1]

It should be clear why "Be reasonable" sometimes has the force of "Be accommodating to the views, or to the interests, of others." The idea even filters down to pricing. A "reasonable" price is an accommodating one. In all of this, we need to see that what is reasonable has no significant connection with the core sense of "reason." Rather it is a matter of social or practical intelligence.

Reason in the core sense in fact is compatible with many forms of stupidity. Remember that reason tells us that if Socrates is a man, and all men are mortal, then Socrates must be mortal. Reason tells us equally that if Socrates is a turkey, and all turkeys have the size of an entire galaxy, then Socrates has the size of an entire galaxy. It is always true of reason in the core sense that the quality of the conclusions depends on the quality of the starting points of the reasoning. As computer programmers used to say, "Garbage in, garbage out."

Even more to the point, reason in the core sense represents exceptionally crisp, very secure moves from starting points to conclusions. In deductive reasoning the conclusions thus can be certain if the starting points are true; in inductive reasoning the conclusions can be probable. The Oxford philosopher Gilbert Ryle once remarked that the processes of reason in this narrow sense were to what we call reasoning in ordinary thought and life much like what military parades are to actual military

1. *Mencius,* trans. D. C. Lau (Harmondsworth: Penguin Books, 1970), Book IV, B. 16, 130.

operations. Reasoning in ordinary thought and practical decisions is not
so crisp and secure.

Perhaps it is not justified to speak of "reasoning" in much of the
workings of intelligence in everyday life? Sometimes we do consciously reflect and weigh reasons that may eventually lead to conclusions. But
often we simply make a judgment, and this can be a truncated process
especially if there is very little time. Maybe later, if someone asks us to
explain why we said or did such-and-such, we might piece together the
kind of justification that originally could have led us (if we had taken
the time and the thought) to our judgment. When there is reflection, it
often does look like there is reasoning, although even then the reasoning is typically irregular (by the standards of logic texts) and does not
conform to reason in the core sense. Where there isn't prior reflection,
we still might want to say that there had been implicit (or unconscious)
reasoning.

Either way, this is not reason in the core sense. Suppose though that we
were to decide that the reasoning of ordinary life qualifies as "reason" in
some extended sense. Does it exclude emotion? Might emotions sometimes play a positive role in these processes? In order to be clear about
this, we need to revisit the topic of the emotions (see Appendix, Number
5), and look at how they might function in intelligent reflection.

## Emotions

It is easy to confuse emotion with feeling. Usually there is some connection. Emotions very often involve a component of feeling. Further, this
element is often quite noticeable and has a considerable effect on the tex-
tures of our lives. Because of this, many early accounts of emotions treated them as merely feelings.

As long as emotions are thought of as feelings, and strong feelings capture our attention, it is possible to think of emotions as magical retreats
from engagement with reality. Emotions like anger, fear, love, and hope, in
this view, impose a vision of the world—guided by affect and inclination,
panic, or despair—significantly different from the matter-of-fact image
that might allow us to cope.

No doubt this often happens, and it is part of the case against strong emotions. But it is very one-sided as an account of how emotions work in our lives. A balanced account becomes possible once we are more clear about what emotions are, and also about the range of emotional states.

The Appendix, Number 5, summarizes a revolution in the last thirty or forty years, both in psychology and in philosophy, in accounts of what emotions are. A dramatic set of experiments by Schachter and Singer showed that an induced feeling could be reported as a variety of emotions, depending on the narrative scenario that surrounded the feeling.[2] Psychologists and philosophers who adopted an analytical attitude could see that a central element of emotions, at least typically, was a judgment. The judgment could be true or false. Anger, for example, can make sense if someone really has behaved badly. If the object of the anger has not behaved badly, though, the anger simply is a mistake.

When we are fully aware of our emotions, we are aware of the judgments that they typically contain. In explaining our anger, we might say "Did you see what he did? It's intolerable." Notoriously people in love enjoy thinking about the lovable qualities of the beloved, which in some sense justify the love.

Emotions however often develop by stages, beginning as inclinations or inchoate feelings, such that the person having them may be barely aware of them. A first stage of love, for example, might be an ill-understood inclination to seek the company of so-and-so. Perhaps there is a judgment implicit in this, as there usually is in the first flush of anger. But the judgment can seem veiled or ambiguous for a while, and the immediate awareness (if there is any) is likely to be of the inclination or the feeling.

Some emotions, when they are fully formed, typically center on what looks like a judgment of value. Let me explain what I mean by a judgment of value, or value judgment. These phrases can have more than one meaning; in this book they are used (except when otherwise indicated) with a specific, narrow meaning. There is a broad sense in which they stand for judgments either of whether behavior is to be recommended or avoided, or of whether something should be desired or avoided (that is,

---

2. See Stanley Schachter and Jerome Singer, from "Cognitive, Social, and Physiological Determinants of Emotional State," in *What Is an Emotion?*, eds. Cheshire Calhoun and Robert Solomon (New York: Oxford University Press, 1984), 172–83.

regarded as a possible reward or as possible bad luck). The central concern of this book though is with *value in the narrow sense* of what is rewarding or unrewarding in itself in the context in which it occurs, apart from causal consequences.

Context is part of this because some things are more desirable or dreadful in some contexts than in others. The phrase "in itself" represents a classic distinction between something being good in itself (for its own sake) and it being good as a means to something else. Happiness is often taken as a prime example of something that is good, first and foremost, for its own sake. Money is a good example of something that most of us would think is good, not in itself, but rather primarily as a means to the satisfactions that it makes possible.

Examples of emotions that center on judgments of value (in my narrow sense) are delight, admiration, envy, pity, distaste, and disgust. We can get a clearer picture if we examine each of these. We will want to look in each both for the place of judgment of value in the fully formed, self-conscious forms of the emotion, and also at how opening stages of the emotion might point toward such judgments.

In this survey we should be wary of overgeneralizing. One needs an eye for diversity. Not all emotions are alike. Often there are significant differences even among cases of the same emotion.

The place of value judgment in delight, for example, varies considerably. Sometimes we are prepared not to like something, perhaps because it seems strange or repugnant or we have heard unfavorable comments on it, but then it seems really marvelous to us. We delight in it. Sometimes the judgment is merely that the experience is very nice, one that we really enjoy. There is no tendency then to assign very high value to the object or the experience, as pleasant as it is. It is not one of the highpoints of life. In other cases, though, the judgment may be that the experience (and perhaps also the object that produced it) is truly of outstanding value.

In short, a range of possibilities goes from "It's delightful if you like that kind of thing" or "I don't know why; it just appealed to me in a funny way," all the way to "That is really great, the highpoint of this period of my life" and "That is a really good piece of music/painting/film, that offers something wonderful to anyone that appreciates it." Sometimes, a relevant variable is how idiosyncratic one's delight is felt to be. Certainly things that one thinks are likely to seem delightful (or at least *should* seem delightful) continuing over some time, to a fair number of people, are usually ones that provide experiences that are the objects of favorable value judgments, which will be part of the delight. These alternatives may be latent in the opening stage of delight. Often, it seems to me, the beginning of delight involves a sense of surprise. What is delightful may not have been anticipated. The surprise can seem, in some cases, like a tickle. Sometimes there is a sense of something impressive coming into view. In that event we are likely to have at least a tentative sense of positive value (both of the experience, and of what provides it), especially if it looks like what provides the experience could continue to be rewarding.

Admiration is unlike delight in that there are no plausible cases in which it might seem like a tickle. When we begin to admire something or someone's life, there may be an element of surprise. By and large, we do not admire anything unless we think it better than ordinary. By definition, most of what we expect to encounter will be at the level of the ordinary. So it often must be the case that we are prepared for something ordinary, and find ourselves instead beginning to admire what we encounter. Typically, the favorable judgment will be there from the beginning. This is again unlike delight; we can experience an opening stage of delight before sorting out whether it warrants an especially favorable judgment of value.

Envy on the face of it should involve a favorable judgment of value, specifically of something that the envied person has. Why should one envy someone if whatever he or she has seems worthless? This neat analysis however does not do justice to the variety of envy.

Recall that human life is full of ambivalence. Often we have a strongly positive attitude toward something which, on reflection, we are inclined to think of as worthless or worse. (An alcoholic might think this way about getting drunk.) Even after the reflection, the strongly positive attitude remains. Occasionally, as in the case of phobias or irrational dread, we have a strong negative attitude toward things that on reflection we think not particularly negative in their values.

That for which we most keenly envy people is usually glittering and superficial. Someone who sincerely believes that the most important value in life is, say, peace of mind, might say "I envy you" to someone who appears to have achieved peace of mind—and might mean it. But this envy is likely not to be of the keen, bothersome sort. There may well be sharper envy of people who are wealthy, win prestigious prizes, or have apparently exciting relationships with attractive partners, even if the considered view of the person who envies is that *these* things are much less important than peace of mind.

It is almost as if there are two people within the one who envies. One of them is mature and reflective, and deeply discounts any desires that would be more characteristic perhaps of someone who is young and unsophisticated. The other one to some extent retains these desires. Perhaps we are almost all like this?

This suggests a complicated story of the development of a particular emotion of envy. No doubt in some cases the feelings of envy become stronger with time. Bloggs may start out by mildly resenting Smurf's wealth and success. But then, particularly if Bloggs' own career is going nowhere, this might prey on his mind, and the feelings of envy could become very strong indeed. It might become increasingly difficult for Bloggs to resist the judgment that the wealth and success which Smurf enjoys really do have considerable positive value, and that this is why he (Bloggs) wants such things.

On the other hand, Bloggs might be reasonably happy about his own circumstances, and have a mature, reflective attitude toward what is important in life. The development of Bloggs' envy of Smurf then might go as follows. Bloggs starts with a strong feeling of envy: Smurf's wealth and success (as compared with his own) really bother him. It naturally occurs to him that the feeling makes sense only if the wealth and success genuinely are important. A positive value judgment to that effect appears to be implicit in Bloggs' envy. But Bloggs' considered opinion (in this version of the story) is that the value judgment actually overstates the importance of conspicuous wealth and success. This does not make the feelings of envy entirely go away, but it considerably dampens their strength.[3]

Pity might seem like the negative counterpart of envy. Envy grows out

---

3. Much of my discussion of envy reflects a tendency to agree with Nietzsche's sense that, by and large, envy should be an unwanted emotion. Here as elsewhere, though, one should not generalize too swiftly. There are some cases in which envy is both justified and in some broad sense rational (although even in those cases it can be damaging if dwelled upon). The most poignant ones center on opportunities: chances for a good education, access to a fulfilling career, or opportunities for close and satisfying personal relationships. Those of us who are lucky in life, including the luck of having been born in liberal, prosperous societies, may underestimate how enviable our lives are in such respects.

of attraction to whatever it is that someone else has (and you don't); pity
grows out of feelings of repugnance to what someone else has (and in
most cases is presumed not to have wanted) and you do not. Both emotions bring out the comparative nature of judgments of well-being. Envy
makes you feel not as well off as you otherwise might have felt. Pity makes
you feel better off. Because of this, both can look unwholesome. Envy can
sour appreciation of what might be, in most respects, a rather fortunate
life. Pity can contain an unsavory overtone of gloating over the fact that
you are not as badly off as so-and-so.

One respect in which pity is not merely the negative counterpart of
envy is this. Envy often expresses a shallow attraction to glittering rewards
which, when we have time to think, we would reflectively judge to have
little or no value. Hence, we often do not want to endorse the kind of
value judgment that is implicit in envy. It would be extremely rare though
for us reflectively to judge that the value judgment implicit in pity was a
mistake.

This is because part of us can long for things that would appeal to a
rather stupid, primitive person, and that (perhaps) we think we know are
worth not all that much. But most of the things that would seem damaging to a rather stupid, primitive person are things that we believe really are
damaging. We pity people because they are seriously ill, or are in great
pain, or have had close personal relationships fall apart, or have lost their
money or their reputation or opportunities for professional success. By
and large these are things that we do think are lamentable.

There can be cases in which someone has intensely valued something
that we think is trivial or worthless, and then loses it and is seriously upset.
If we focus on what was lost we typically do not feel pity. (The loss in a
certain light might seem comical. Suppose Smurf loses a much adored
glass case that contained a fingernail reported to have belonged to a
famous pop star. Some people might be amused.) If on the other hand,
we focus on the distress of the person who has the sense of loss, we could
feel pity, but this would include the judgment that such distress really was
a negative experience.

In short, the judgment implicit in the first stirrings of pity (that the
pitiable person has suffered something that genuinely has significant negative value) usually does persist. Reflection on the values involved is
much less likely to undermine pity than in the case of envy. Hence, by
and large the first stirrings of pity amount to an awareness of negative

value within someone's else's life, an awareness that typically then becomes explicit.

Distaste also can begin as a stirring of feeling, in which a judgment of negative value is merely latent. The first hint of distaste may be a sense of uneasiness or an aversion to something. What is implicit is usually not a negative judgment, but rather a question mark hovering over the object of the uneasiness. We might say, "I don't know why this bothers me." But there is a suspicion of something negative.

A settled distaste may not move past this point. There may be no more than the judgment that suspicion is appropriate, that perhaps something is faulty. The value judgments inherent in various emotions do not have to be of the straightforward "Yes" or "No" sorts. They can express doubt, or the thought that something might be very good (but it is hard to be sure) or very bad (but perhaps time will tell).

Alternatively, distaste may involve a progression from doubt and suspicion to a definite judgment that the object of distaste has very little (or negative) value. Are such judgments reliable? Often they are not. In general it would be a mistake to suppose that judgments of value inherent in various emotions can't be mistaken, or even that they always have some degree of plausibility.

Distaste is often the result of prejudice against persons or practices or objects of a certain sort. Frequently the prejudice represents a traditional cultural attitude that has very little to be said for it, but nevertheless retains a hold over many people. The object can be a kind of social relation (e.g., interracial dating somewhere where it previously had been unknown), or even gastronomic experiences such as eating raw fish.

All of this needs to be said, but also that what holds in various cases does not necessarily hold in every case. Not all distaste is the product of upbringing or prejudice. Sometimes upbringing and general cultural influences predispose us to think well of certain practices or persons, but then in actual experience we discover feelings of distaste. The occasional Southerner before the Civil War who came to feel that slavery was wrong would have a story like that. In various cultures there have been instances of people who, suddenly and almost unaccountably, came to feel distaste for traditional practices that they then judged to be cruel. Distaste often represents cultural programming, but it sometimes looks like a dawning awareness of what decent behavior would be like.

One might think at first of disgust as merely an intensified form of distaste. There is a sharper connection sometimes between disgust and the power of ideas associated with the object of disgust. In one experiment, psychologists placed a cockroach in a glass, and then washed and sterilized the glass. Even after the glass was washed and sterilized, many subjects refused to drink from it. It was too disgusting.[4]

Also, disgust is often directed at violation of taboos. Many taboos have to do with sex, including acts that some people regard as inherently disgusting. In cultures with food taboos, similar disgust can be felt for acts of eating forbidden food.

It goes without saying that judgments that something is disgusting generally are debatable. The word "taboo" has associations with primitive superstition. But here (as elsewhere in this book) I would urge caution in generalizing from what is arguably true in many cases to what then is assumed to be of course true in all cases.

There may be cases in which taboos rest on basic psychological attitudes (including, say, those toward matters of life and death), which we undermine at our peril. This includes incest taboos, but perhaps the most plausible candidates are taboos related to treatment of the dead. One was probed in a Monty Python skit in which a young man approaches a funeral director, asking about a cheap way of disposing of the body of his mother, who has just died. What is recommended is gross (including cannibalism), and at that point the skit turns upon itself as disgusting.

Imagine a society in which people can sign consent forms saying "You can do anything you like with my body after I die," and in which corpses might be used as, say, garden ornaments or Halloween decorations. This, like the Monty Python skit, is something that most people would find disgusting. The disgust looks like a primitive response. But can we dismiss it as merely that? There is the worrying thought that any society that did not find such things disgusting would have become really callous, and perhaps lacking in respect for manifestations of human individuals. The taboo in this case might have an important cultural and psychological function.

Some of this is speculative, but at the least is an argument for thinking further instead of seeking intellectual closure. In general, disgust, like other emotions related to how we should behave or what we should

---

4. See Paul Rozin, Jonathan Haidt, and Clark R. McCauley, "Disgust," in *Handbook of Emotions,* eds. M. Lewis and J. M. Haviland (New York: Guilford Press, 1993), 575–94.

value, is in some cases a very unreliable indicator and in others can be revelatory. Examples of the latter can be found in ways in which human
beings sometimes treat other human beings—especially ways that trample
on any sense of human dignity—that really are disgusting. The growing
feeling of disgust that you might have quickly yields a negative judgment,
one that in the cases just mentioned is arguably the appropriate one.

## Following the "Reason" Option

How most of us actually arrive at judgments of value is one thing. How we
think we ought to arrive at them may be quite another. The ideology of
"be rational" can distort both our view of the actual process, and also our
sense of what we should be doing. Certainly there are people who will try
to be overtly "rational" in arriving at judgments of value. Often (especially
among philosophers) this can result in using general formulas for what must
have value, and trying to construct a model of values using these.

General formulas are not always worthless. The general formula that a
desirable kind of life is a happy one has some merit. If someone is unhappy, we would normally think that this detracts from the quality of his or
her life. But our discussion in Chapter 2 creates a strong case for saying
that happy people (e.g., happy idiots, happy sadists) do not always have
lives that we should envy or think desirable, and also for thinking that an
exceptionally high degree of happiness would entail unwholesome smugness and complacency. It is highly misleading to hold that quality of a life
correlates closely with the degree of happiness.

We generally would be reluctant, it is true, to consider the life of
someone who was thoroughly miserable as enviable. But someone who is
in the middle of the scale between happiness and unhappiness—not really happy, but not really unhappy either—might have strong positive features in her or his life that would justify regarding that life as enviable and
desirable on the whole.

The formula that links happiness and desirability of life has merit in
that there usually is a connection, and sometimes the connection looks
strong. But if read as disclosing inflexible rules of human life, it fails. A
similar point can be made about any generalization that links personal
accomplishment with the desirability of a life.

There are all sorts of reasons why personal accomplishment generally contributes to the quality of a life. Most accomplishments involve sustained exercise of skills, which typically involve the highly desirable pleasures of "flow." They also typically are sources of pride, which can contribute to a sense of self that matters to happiness. Personal relations also can be enhanced, and there can be other rewards.

But it is possible to have considerable personal accomplishments and yet, for various reasons, to be thoroughly miserable. Other things can go seriously wrong in a life that contains personal accomplishments. Because of all of this, any generalization that links personal accomplishments to the desirability or enviability of a life should be read as at best a guideline, rather than an inflexible rule. It needs to be understood with qualifiers such as "usually" or "by and large."

Hence reasoning (in the very extended sense of "reasoning") in the abstract about what makes lives desirable and enviable, while it can be useful, has its limitations. There also is a fundamental problem for someone who wants to regard this territory as governed by "reason." Where do we get the starting points of any "reasoning" about the connections between a good life and happiness or personal accomplishment? Some experience of happiness (and of lack of happiness) and of personal accomplishment, and of the difference it can make to the felt quality of life, surely is relevant. The starting points, in short, require judgments of value, that ideally grow out of personal experience and are crystallized in emotions, and in any case cannot be viewed as *a priori* truths.

Anyone who doubts that emotions which crystallize judgments of value are fundamental to any reasoning about value should ask herself or himself this question. Could we think about what is desirable or enviable in life if nothing ever seemed delightful or admirable, and nothing ever was seen as pitiable, distasteful, or disgusting? It is very hard to imagine a world that was absolutely without emotions in which we (or the stick figures that would have our places) would make value judgments.

The argument here is highly consonant with the seventeenth-century French philosopher Blaise Pascal's well-known claim that "The heart has reasons that reason knows not." Pascal was principally concerned with religious knowledge, and our concern here is different: it is with our sense of what makes a life really desirable or the reverse. But the argument is parallel. Inputs exist that should have weight, that are not from anything that could be called "reason." Specifically, a basis for various kinds of judgments of what is desirable is provided by developing emotions and not by reason.

What we absorb from these inputs then can take the form of "reasons." These can be used in reasoning (in the extended sense of "reasoning") about what has value. This chapter fits this pattern.

It cannot too strongly be emphasized that everything in this process could involve mistakes. Envy can be of what any judicious onlooker would think worthless and other emotions (such as admiration, distaste, and disgust) can be highly suggestible and unreliable. Any emotional response can be flawed or a mistake. This seems especially likely when the emotions are, as it were, not first-hand but rather merely represent acculturation or upbringing.

That we often think we should discount the indications of other people's emotions, and sometimes those of our own emotions, does not mean that such discounting is always appropriate. Some emotional responses can be revelatory of value, and can be judged as such by people who are judicious and have considerable relevant experience of life. That such judgments always remain contestable does not mean that they cannot, at least sometimes, be trusted.

The reasoning process, which takes off from starting points provided by emotional experience, also is a blunt and not entirely reliable instrument. Philosophy in particular should never be viewed as oracular. Some degree of distrust is always appropriate. Apart from this general caution, there needs to be special caution in relation to reasoning about what is desirable or enviable in life. Reasoning will use general terms, and we need to be mindful of the possibilities of significant variation among the items or cases covered by any general term. Nuances in forms of life, social settings, or experiences can make a crucial difference in value, even though the nuances can be extremely difficult to capture in language.

Cautions sounded above apply to judgments of value needed to provide starting points of any reasoning about value, and sometimes apply to the reasoning process itself. It may appear from all this that a degree of skepticism of judgments of value is always warranted. Is making judgments of value a hopeless enterprise?

A short answer is that it is never entirely secure, but often is not hopeless. Sometimes we can have grounds for a considerable degree of confidence that a judgment of what is desirable and enviable in life is an acceptable one. The most favorable cases concern particular judgments of value (i.e., judgments of value in relation to a particular life or case) that grow out of personal experience. This will be taken up in the final chapter of this book.

## Conclusion

Emotions, rather than some faculty of reason, typically provide the starting points of our judgments of what is important in a good life. Also, such judgments can take the form of emotional responses. In some cases inchoate emotions will appear as the first phase in a process in which judgments of value only gradually take shape. In others, the judgments are fully formed as an element in the first appearance of the emotion.

Gaining an appreciation of the things that are important is to a large extent an education of the emotions. As both Aristotle and Confucian philosophers insisted, it is crucial to have the right emotions about what comes up in life. The process of arriving at this capacity requires experience and sensitivity, but many philosophers have argued that it also requires training of our responses so that they are not dominated by primitive and strong emotions. Milder emotions—such as delight, distaste, admiration, and compassion—often are more reliable guides to values, and usually also lead to more effective behavior. This again is an area in which changing the self can be of great importance.

# Myth Five

## THERE IS NO REAL CONNECTION, AT LEAST IN THIS LIFE, BETWEEN TRUE VIRTUE AND A DESIRABLE KIND OF LIFE

Nice guys, according to Leo Durocher (who was manager of the old Brooklyn Dodgers), finish last. It may look obvious that winners are people who cut corners and break the rules. The amiable types are also-rans. So what is clearer than that there is no positive connection between virtue and having a desirable life?

Unless this is a huge mistake. Is virtue the same as being nice? We need to think about what virtue is, and also about what it is to be nice.

Virtue involves behaving well in matters of importance, even when tempted or under great pressure. In traditional societies, a "virtuous woman" was one who would not yield to the temptations to which women were thought most vulnerable. In much this spirit, one could speak of a "virtuous accountant" as one who would never be caught up in an accounting scandal. To be a virtuous person, one presumably needs a high general standard of behavior, come what may.

Niceness typically involves a degree of amiability and charm, advanced social skills, and perhaps some small acts of considerateness. Nice people are usually easy to get along with, and that is one of the reasons why most of us tend to like them. Is this a large part of virtue? Could someone be virtuous and not a nice person?

In asking whether virtue contributes to having a desirable kind of life, we need to think about what makes a life rewarding. Winning a championship and making a lot of money are certainly appealing. But are there more important things?

This chapter applies philosophical therapy to a perennial myth which draws on two attractive ideas. One is that niceness either is virtue or is a large part of it. Another is that what people generally desire, and envy in other people's lives, has considerable value. If we put these two seductive ideas together, it looks clear that nice, virtuous people often do not do well in life. They often get little of what most people keenly desire.

Even if we put niceness to the side and concentrate on virtue, it is clear that there are virtuous people whose lives are not, by the standards of most people, at all enviable. Virtue is compatible with constant disappointment and extreme pain. Does true virtue make it less likely these will occur in your life? Perhaps. But we also need to consider whether the values that make a life worth living include a great deal that is less obvious than pain and disappointment.

## Deeper Values?

That there are less obvious values and that they contribute greatly to the quality of a life is a running theme in much classical Greek, Indian, and Chinese philosophy. Well-known philosophers for whom this was central include Plato, Aristotle, and Confucius. Plato and Confucius, in particular, emphasize the great value of a harmony in your emotional structures.

Their views may at first seem counterintuitive. But they can look plausible. Start from the fact that most people value greatly a variety of things they can get and keep, or a variety of relationships. We keep wanting more, and we want to keep what we have. This is the normal human condition.

This gives life a mixed character. There are pleasures, but there also is a perennial undercurrent of dissatisfaction (because there is so much we want that we don't have), and of anxiety (because we might lose what we have, or fail in our next attempts to get things).

Further there can be inner conflicts, because we may find ourselves wanting things which we could not get without violating social norms. We want to stay out of trouble. But really it would be nice to have those things.

Because of all of this, people's normal life is unfocused as our minds move from one desire to another. It also is conflicted, because some of our desires (such as the desire to stay out of trouble and have good relations with people) are at cross-purposes with other desires. Plato in particular views this as a low grade mental illness. In modern terms it is like neurosis. Part of being neurotic is that your various activities and wishes trip over each other. Plato would think that this is true of the great majority of people, although at a level at which it is often not classified as a psychological problem, because it is so common.

As Confucius sees it, the great majority of people are too anxious. They also are too concerned with luck. This is because the things that they think are most important in life, such as money and reputation, are very subject to luck.

In effect, both philosophers hold that robust mental health is rarer than you might think. Harmonious emotional structures are required. These are, in their views, more deeply gratifying than the things that most of us tend to want most.

What does this have to do with virtue? Confucius, Plato, and Aristotle all believe that the practice of virtue is intimately connected with what it is that you want and that you enjoy. The truly virtuous person, in their views, is not merely someone who happens to do the right things. To be truly virtuous, you have to be someone who enjoys and feels thoroughly at home in doing the right thing. Your personal values—what you find most rewarding—will center on being the kind of person for whom virtue has become second nature. Confucius and Aristotle in particular think that you can "get into" being virtuous in a way that makes virtuous actions deeply pleasant to you.

This points toward a sense of life's rewards that looks very different from merely wanting to win, be rich, or be popular. The great ancient philosophers all contend that the psychological rewards of being the right sort of person loom so large that, even if you lose your money and reputation, you would still be at least fairly well off.

If this argument works at all, it will be because of a sharp separation between, on one hand, what many of us want and most sharply envy in other people's lives, and, on the other hand, what turns out (in actual experience and reflection) to be most worthwhile. In the last chapter we explored ways in which envy is often of the glittering and superficial. It can represent the values of an immature corner of the person who envies, and not that person's considered values. In much the same way, many of us do find ourselves wanting things that, on reflection, we are far from sure would be good for us.

Confucius at one point remarked that he never met a man who loves virtue as much as he loves female beauty.[1] This can be taken as a comment on a split in virtually everyone (including himself in youth and middle age) between what generates a strong immediate pull on one hand, and what might be reflectively preferred on the other. Plato's vision of the division of the soul (in the *Republic,* the *Phaedrus,* and elsewhere) points in a similar direction.

If we accept the values of the immature self that envies and wants the flashy, then there is no reason to assume a strong connection between a person's virtue and how good will be the life that this person will have. We then could imagine someone who is genuinely virtuous but whose luck is bad enough to ruin the quality of her or his life. If instead we accept the values of a mature self, do we get a radically different image of someone whose quality of life is largely impervious to luck? Plato, Aristotle, and Confucius all think so.

Cases presented in the great books of the world are a little (but not entirely) like these two possibilities. One is Job in the Bible, a very good man who loses everything that he values (children and possessions) and also develops a plague of boils, so that his life is simply wretched, despite his great virtue. This is not exactly bad luck, but is portrayed instead as a test of Job's virtue under pressure which God allows the Adversary to conduct. Further, what Job loses is not exactly flashy, but the material wealth and children do represent values that virtually anyone would immediately recognize, as does Job's extreme physical discomfort. A message of the *Book of Job* is that God's justice here on earth is so different from human justice that it will be unintelligible to us; someone as virtuous as Job can have a life that goes really bad, and the reassuring and simplistic explanations given by his friends are to be rejected.[2]

A different view expressed here and there in classical Greek literature is personified in Oedipus and in King Priam of Troy. King Priam lived to see the invading Greeks destroy his city and kill his sons. Seemingly everything that he cared for became a disaster. Nothing in

---

1. *Analects of Confucius,* trans. Edward Slingerland (Indianapolis: Hackett Publishing Co., 2003), Book IX.18, 92. Arthur Waley, for whom the passage is Book IX.17, translates this as "whose desire to build up his moral power was as strong as sexual desire" instead of "loves virtue as much as he loves female beauty."

2. See *Job,* Chapter 38ff.

Homer's *Iliad* contradicts the assumption that he was highly virtuous, yet at the end we might consider that his life had become miserable rather than desirable.

So we might think. But Aristotle, in his *Nicomachean Ethics,* presents Priam as a test case of the connection between virtue and *eudaemonia* (a Greek word that is generally translated as "happiness," but seems to mean something closer to "well-being"). He contends that while Priam's misfortunes did lower his level of *eudaemonia,* it still remained in the intermediate range.[3]

Oedipus is a well-known character with drastically bad luck. He was abandoned as a child, and as an adult journeyed to his birthplace. Unbeknownst to him, the older man who started a fight with him on the road—a fight in which Oedipus killed the other man—was his father. Unbeknownst to him, the attractive older woman whom he then married was his mother. When all of this was revealed, Oedipus, in a moment of agony, put out his own eyes. He survived to go into exile and be led by the hand by his daughters.

As portrayed by Sophocles, Oedipus had great virtues despite all this. In *Oedipus at Colonnus,* which presents him at the end of his life, Oedipus repeatedly affirms his essential innocence. Although he remains under pressure, the portrayal can be read as marked by self-acceptance and a degree of happiness.[4]

It is not totally clear if King Priam and Oedipus were actual people, and we don't know much about them if they were. What about real people about whom we do know? Here are two examples of a combination of great virtue and a degree of what might seem like bad luck in life.

One is Socrates, who is portrayed in many of the dialogues of Plato and also in reminiscences written by Xenophon. Socrates himself almost certainly would have denied that he had had bad luck; but that in itself shows something. Suppose that you think you have a good life, despite what most people would consider bad luck. Then you are likely to deny

---

3. See Aristotle, *The Nicomachean Ethics,* trans. Terence Irwin, Second Edition (Indianapolis: Hackett Publishing Co., 1999), 1101a, 14. In 1100a, 12, Aristotle sounds a little less positive, but all the same regards the values in Priam's life as not in the low range.

4. Albert Camus (*The Myth of Sisyphus,* trans. Justin O'Brien [New York: Vintage Books, 1955], 90) makes a point of quoting Oedipus' judgment that "All is well" in a final discussion of happiness.

that it really was bad luck—because in your view it did not harm you in any significant way.

Many people would consider it bad luck to be as poor as Socrates was. Socrates also did not seem to get on well with his wife, Xantippe; some people might think that it was bad luck that he didn't have a spouse that appreciated him.[5] The biggest piece of what most people would consider bad luck, though, was the following. At the end, Socrates' habit of asking difficult questions had irritated so many of his fellow citizens that he was condemned to death on what were essentially trumped-up charges. He was forced to swallow poison. It is abundantly clear, though, that Socrates was thoroughly happy about the quality of his life from start to finish.

Another real-life combination of great virtue with what many people would take to be bad luck was Confucius. We think of him as a great philosopher and an example of ancient wisdom. His personal goals though centered on social and political reforms in China that would focus on devoting resources to the well-being of the people. He believed that this could be accomplished if one of the kingdoms that remained of the old empire instituted good government, and became a demonstration model of what a society ruled by virtue would be like. In this pursuit, he traveled from kingdom to kingdom, accompanied by his students, hoping somewhere to be appointed as a high official. Then he could put his ideas into practice.

Great effort and much persuasion in various courts went into this. In the end he failed. It seems likely that he died thinking of himself as a failure. A story in the *Analects* (the account of Confucius compiled by his students and their students and students' students) tells of a time when he was very ill and near death. His disciples dressed themselves up as retainers of a high official. They may have thought of this as both a mark of respect and a consolation. But when Confucius came to, he was upset and ordered the robes to be taken away.[6]

---

5. But then we don't have Xantippe's point of view, really. For an imaginative reconstruction, see Bertolt Brecht, "Socrates Wounded," in *Collected Stories*, eds. John Willett and Ralph Mannheim (New York: Arcade/Little, Brown, 1998), 139–53.

6. *Analects* Book IX.12, 90. Confucius' persistent desire for the opportunities of high office is made clear in IX.13, and his regret at never having been given a chance is expressed in IX.7.

Seemingly this is a combination of great virtue and bad luck—failure in the most fundamental goal of one's life. But Confucius reportedly claimed that to have real virtues is to be largely impervious to bad luck. His view, like Aristotle's, was that to be really virtuous guarantees at least a moderately high quality of life. In this they both oppose the view of the *Book of Job*.

This needs to be put in perspective. Things we care about in life are not all of the same sort. Some are, as it were, closer to the bone.

One way to see this is to distinguish between two kinds of things you might regard as contributing to the quality of your life. Some are crucial to your sense of self, of who you are. For example, you might think of yourself as someone who would not let down a friend; and this makes you happy about who you are. Other things that we care about look incidental; thus, experiencing the value of such-and-such does not seem to matter much to your sense of self or to what kind of person you are. Experiences of good food and other sensory pleasures might fit this profile. It is true that how you take them, and also how you integrate them in your life, might well depend on the kind of person you are. But the immediacy of the pleasure looks pretty much the same whoever has it.

This is true—perhaps even more so—of many pains. Indeed, there may be a stronger sense of our common humanity in relation to pain than in relation to pleasure, partly because of the greater convergence in just what gives people intense pain. Again, this applies to the immediacy of pain. There can be great variation in how people handle pain. One extreme is represented by people who are trained exceptionally well to have a sense of control while experiencing pain, so that they can escape the passivity associated with suffering. Examples are women giving birth who have been trained to control the experience, and disciplined Buddhists.[7]

The immediacy of pain (if the control is absent) and the immediacy of strong sensory pleasures tends to be impersonal. This may be one of the factors in our keen envy of other people's strong sensory pleasures, and certainly in our pity for others' intense pains. We can imagine ourselves, as the persons we are, with those pleasures or those pains.

7. See Alexandra David-Neel, *Magic and Mystery in Tibet* (New York: Dover Books, 1971), 16.

Satisfactions or forms of pain that are far less impersonal offer a less clear route to envy or pity. Certainly we often feel sorry for people who are in real distress because of psychological conflicts. But our sympathy may well be less keen if we cannot relate what upsets them to anything in our own psychology. It is not as easy as sympathizing with someone who is in intense pain or has just lost a leg.

A theme that runs through most classical Greek, Indian, and Chinese philosophies is that thought and experience can be organized in ways that are very different from those of the average person, and that provide sources of satisfaction that are deep and ongoing. The accounts of what a philosophy considers a superior way of organizing thought and experience vary considerably. Stoic and Epicurean versions differ from those of Plato and Aristotle. Daoist and Confucian views are very different from one another; there is a similar contrast between Buddhist views and those associated with texts such as the *Upanishads* and the *Bhagavad Gita*.

Suppose that we know someone who has implemented one of these versions of a purportedly superior way of organizing thought and experience, and that (rightly or wrongly) we have a sense that it is really working for her or him, that there is an uncommon degree of calm and poise and a high degree of ongoing satisfaction with the quality of everyday life. We could envy that. But the route to envy is much less clear than it is in the case of someone who is a wealthy celebrity with attractive consorts and wonderful homes and cars. This in part is because, in the first case, the source of satisfaction is so inner and personal, having to do with the kind of person into which someone has transformed herself or himself. If we have not absorbed a similar way of organizing our thought and experience, we can hardly substitute ourselves—as we are—in that picture. It is much easier to substitute ourselves in the picture of the celebrity's glamorous lifestyle, and much easier (as we are) to think we have a sense of what it might be like. (In reality, of course, the celebrity's lifestyle might be almost as alien to us as that of the confirmed Buddhist's or Confucian's; but I am talking about appearances and perceptions.)

What might provide an ongoing source of satisfaction in everyday life—one that we *should* envy, if we have any sense of what it would be like? In order to answer this, we need to look at something central to our thought and experience, and also mysterious: the self. Related to this is something arguably crucial to the quality of our ongoing experience: our sense of self.

## Self and Sense of Self

What makes the self peculiarly difficult to talk about is that, arguably, we never experience it in any direct, normal way. This point is made by Buddha, in denying the claim (central to the classic text of Hinduism, the *Upanishads*) that each of us has an *atman,* an inner self. It is also made by the eighteenth century Scottish philosopher David Hume. Both contend that we simply do not experience any psychic element that gives us an unchanging inner nature or personal identity. There is, in the mind, nothing of any importance that stays the same all of the time.

This is very dramatic, and you may look inside yourself to validate the point. Is there something you see that is YOU and that is there all the time? But one critical response has been that something is lacking in the way these two philosophers set up their test. If Buddha and Hume looked for their selves and couldn't find any, what was doing the looking?

Is there a way of getting around this problem and finding the self? A possible tactic, developed by the classical philosophy associated with Hinduism, is to arrive at an experience that is "nondual," in the sense of not involving any contrast between subject (what is looking) and object (what is looked for). Whether this makes sense is a very large and difficult subject, which spills well beyond the confines of this book.[8] Presumably only after (and not during) this special experience, which is held to require sustained self-discipline and meditative practices, can one objectify and think of the inner self.

A less radically controversial way of talking about the self, which does not conflict with the point made by Buddha and Hume, is as follows. One can say, "Perhaps there is no thing-like self." But each of us has patterns of thought and behavior associated with our bodies. These developing tendencies in a person amount to the construction of what one could call a "self." Hume follows this path in the second book of his *Treatise of Human Nature* (after rejecting the thing-like self), and there is a similar move in the early Buddhist text *The Questions of King Milinda.*

---

8. See my *Classic Asian Philosophy: A Guide to the Essential Texts* (New York: Oxford University Press, 2001), Chapter 1.

To speak of the "self" in the sense of a constructed self differs from speaking of it as a thing-like constant internal presence. One difference is that the constructed self is always, at least in theory, open to change. It is sometimes said that people "never change," but of course everyone does; it is just that that the continuities are often far more conspicuous than the differences. There can be basic ways in which a great many people do not change much.

Occasionally someone does dramatically and suddenly change her or his pattern of thought and behavior. However, it is generally accepted that drastic changes are not altogether common, and that when they do occur it is more often than not in a very gradual fashion. Because of this, we usually know the kinds of things to expect from the people we know well, even if the certainty is never one hundred percent.

Against this background, we can see that mature, reasonably stable people can have some knowledge of their (constructed) selves. A point that the French philosopher Jean-Paul Sartre repeatedly made is that, if they are honest, they will also think, "I don't have to be like this. I can change." This is consistent with Hume's observation that, even if one chooses to change, it is typically not possible as an immediate result of an effort of will, but rather will be a gradual process of modification, best facilitated by changes in the circumstances of life.[9] It is also consistent with the possibility of real knowledge of how you have been up to now. Sartre's example is the case in which he sits down to rest during a hike. Anyone who knows him and his attitude towards his body could have predicted that he would do that.[10]

You can know the kind of person you have been up until now. It is not easy. Some people, perhaps as a result of demeaning personal relationships, may see themselves in the worst possible light. Probably most of us, in contrast, view who we are in an excessively favorable light. A striking psychological study concludes that the one group that tends to have a fairly accurate view of its aptitudes and capacities consists of people suffering

9. See David Hume, "The Skeptic," in *Essays,* ed. Eugene Miller (Indianapolis: Liberty Fund, 1985), 169ff.

10. Jean-Paul Sartre, *Being and Nothingness,* trans. Hazel Barnes (New York: Philosophical Library, 1956), 453 ff. See also my "Character and Self-Knowledge," *Proceedings of the Aristotelian Society* 85 (1984–5), 219–38.

from severe depression.[11] It may be that many of us think of ourselves as above average in areas in which we are average.

Be that as it may, almost all of us have (or can have) what amounts to a sense of self. What role does this sense of self have in having a good life? Clearly it can be considerable. As we saw in Chapter 2 a major factor in someone's happiness is that person's feeling about herself or himself. This strongly suggests that a sense of one's self as virtuous increases the likelihood of happiness for most people (who would like to feel good about themselves, and would rather not feel guilty).

This seems a plausible generalization. But consider the exceptions. Someone could really like the idea of not being virtuous. They could have real pride in being the most wicked person in a given area. Even in that case, though, residual ideas of decency and of how other people really ought to be treated might mar happiness.

The discussion in Chapter 2 strongly suggests that we can assume that happiness is by and large a major positive feature in a life, even if there are cases in which we tend to discount its value (because of what it is based upon). Hence, the apparent correlation between virtuousness and a high degree of happiness should be treated as a provisional finding about one connection between virtue and the good life.

Nevertheless, it should be treated with caution, for a number of reasons. We have already noted that cases vary. Not only might some people enjoy being "bad," but it also is sadly true that someone who is virtuous might still (for other reasons) not like herself or himself. Any correlation between a sense of self-as-virtuous and the good life must allow for such cases. A correlation, even one that is a *strong* connection, is not necessarily anything like a *uniform* connection.

Another reason for caution is as follows. What is doing the work, at this point, is a person's sense of personal virtue (or its opposite). This sense can be distorted. Some people may find too much fault with themselves, for lapses here or there, or alternatively may exaggerate their own virtue. There

11. See Nico Frijda, "Moods, Emotion Episodes, and Emotions," in *Handbook of Emotions,* eds. M. Lewis and J. M. Haviland (New York: Guilford Press, 1993), 395b–396a; L. B. Alloy and L. Y. Abramson, "Judgment of Contingency in Depressed and Nondepressed Subjects. Sadder But Wiser?" *Journal of Experimental Psychology. General* 108 (1979), 441–85.

can be problems that we have not yet addressed in what constitutes genuine virtue. One possibility, then, is that while some correlation exists between a sense of personal virtue and the good life, there is a further (and perhaps deeper) correlation between the actual possession (or lack of possession) of genuine virtue and the good life. We need to explore this possibility.

## Genuine Virtue

What should count as genuine virtue? Is much of what passes as virtue, by normal community standards, not genuine virtue? This is a large subject, and certainly will not be exhausted in this chapter. In the next chapter we have to consider whether genuine virtue requires a complete absence of moral lapses in one's life, or even whether it requires a strong likelihood that there will be none in the future. Nothing in this chapter will provide definite answers to these questions.

An argument will be offered for setting the standard for genuine virtue higher than that typically represented by normal community standards. In other words, numbers of people who normally seem virtuous really should be reclassified. This seems counterintuitive, but an impressive number of well-known thinkers and writers have suggested this.

One might start with Mark Twain, and his story "The Man That Corrupted Hadleyburg." A town is known for the strict virtue of its leading citizens. Twain makes it clear that a desire to look good is a large part of this "virtue." Someone who resents the town arranges a temptation for these leading citizens. Each one is led to think that he can possess a bag of gold if only he can recall a kind remark made some time previously to a stranger. Remembering the words would identify him as the one who had helped the stranger (and now deserves great reward); at the same time it is arranged that the words are leaked to each of the leading citizens. One after another then claims to have said those words and to have helped the stranger. Plainly these people are not really virtuous. Twain's view is that "The weakest of all weak things is a virtue which has not been tested in the fire."[12]

12. Mark Twain, "The Man That Corrupted Hadleyburg," in *Mark Twain's Short Stories*, ed. Justin Kaplan (New York: Signet Books, 1985), 432.

Corruption at least as serious as what Twain imagined has occurred for real, in many places and in many ways, within the last century. A now classic example in psychology literature is the Milgram experiment, in which the behavior of groups of people, most of whom could have been assumed to have normally behaved in a virtuous way, surprised even the researchers.

In the Milgram experiment, subjects were instructed to administer electric shocks of increasing severity to someone on the other side of a glass partition (who they thought was another experimental volunteer, but actually was an actor) if he failed in certain learning tasks. The actor deliberately kept failing. This led the subjects to administer what they thought were shocks of increasing voltage. Any subject who questioned the procedure, moved by the man's apparent distress, was told "The experiment must go on." More than 60 percent did go on, past the point at which the shocks were supposedly dangerous.

Before we go on to other cases, it might be good to pause to ask just what the Milgram experiment showed. It certainly demonstrated that people in disorienting circumstances, ones in which they might have assumed that there was a proper way of doing things which they did not fully understand (and hence had to take someone else's word), could easily make choices that would have been deeply immoral, had things been as they appeared. Does this mean that these people were not genuinely virtuous, despite prior appearances?

We might hesitate here, for a number of reasons. There is a tradition, even in some matters connected with morality, of people learning from mistakes. Plainly the kind of "mistake" matters. It would seem odd to say of someone "He's OK. He committed only one mass murder, and really he has been staying away from that kind of thing ever since." Some cases though can look a little less straightforward, and wrong actions in these can look as if they have mitigating circumstances.

Perhaps this is true of the Milgram experiments both because of the speed with which they were conducted and because of the oddity of the setting, which some people might have needed more time to think about before proceeding. But we normally do not forgive wrongs merely because the perpetrators were confused and did not have much time in which to decide. The issues here are complex, and will be explored more fully in the next chapter.

It seems less easy to plead mitigating circumstances on behalf of Mark
Twain's characters, who had more time to think and to adjust to whatever was peculiar in their new circumstances. A similar comment applies to
the sizable number of people, during the Nazi occupation of their countries in World War II, who were influenced by fear and a sense of a new
order of things, who therefore collaborated with the brutal agenda of the
Nazis. Wherever there has been a brutal or nasty dictatorship, large numbers of people have behaved immorally, largely to stay out of trouble.
This was true even in ancient Athens during the rule of the Thirty
Tyrants. We are told that five citizens, including Socrates, were ordered to
arrest one Leon of Salamis (presumably an innocent man) and to bring
him to the tyrants (and probable execution). It was a way of implicating
numbers of people in the crimes of the tyrants; to defy their commands
carried obvious risk. Of those who were commanded to arrest Leon of
Salamis, all but one went to seize him. Socrates simply went home. As luck
would have it, on this occasion nothing was done to him.[13]

Living through a brutal dictatorship, or during a very difficult period
in which most people are simply doing what they can in order to survive,
could definitely change one's sense of how many people are genuinely
virtuous. Conversely, in a prosperous, stable, and secure society (like
Hadleyburg before it was corrupted), it is possible to think that the great
majority of people are genuinely virtuous. Anecdotal evidence suggests
that this is a common view among American college students.

There are glimmers of a different point of view at various times in the
past. The German philosopher Gottfried Leibniz, born in 1646 (toward
the end of the brutally devastating Thirty Years War in Germany), is widely portrayed as an optimist. In his *Theodicy*, he argues for the proposition
that God created this world (rather than some other kind of world that
God could have created instead) because this is the best of all possible
worlds. He defends this against what is presented as a likely objection.
How can he say that this is the best of all possible worlds, when more people go to hell than go to heaven?

His reply concedes the premise of the objection. It is true, he says, that
more people go to hell than go to heaven. But the goodness per person
of those who go to heaven is greater than the badness of those who go

---

13. Plato, *Apology*, in *Dialogues of Plato*, trans. B. Jowett (New York: Random House,
1937), St. 32, vol. 1, 415.

to hell. Hence the balance of total goodness minus total badness is positive. This is a window on a view (embodied in the objection, and Leibniz's concession of what it assumes) that clearly would not have included a high estimate of the percentage of the population that was genuinely virtuous.

Plato also would not have given a high estimate. Three places in the *Republic* showed his skepticism about the genuine virtue of most people. The best known is the Myth of the Cave in Book VII, which compares most people's awareness of goodness to the lack of knowledge of people in a cave who see only shadows and never anything in direct light.

Consider also (in Book II) the story of a shepherd who discovers a ring that can make its wearer invisible. We might assume that he previously had behaved virtuously; but it does not take him long to realize that, armed with the ring, he can get away with anything. In the end he commits serious crimes and becomes a tyrant. The insinuation is that virtually everyone would in the end succumb to this temptation, but that Socrates (because of what he values in life) would not.

Finally, there is the story in Book X of the man who has a near-death experience, in which he sees the souls of the recently departed choosing new lives. One of these, who has previously behaved virtuously as a citizen of a well-ordered community, chooses the glittering, evil, and ruinous life of a tyrant. Perhaps this might be surprising, but the suggestion is that his previous "virtue" was a matter of habit but not philosophy.[14]

The fact is that, in a well-regulated society, most of us get used to following the major rules early on. This habit sometimes can be broken if a temptation is sufficiently alluring. But if society is prosperous, stable, and secure, such temptations may not arise all that often for most people.

How much effort has the reader devoted in the last few months to not murdering, raping, torturing, or stealing? For many of us, a normal pattern of generally morally acceptable behavior represents passing a rather easy test.

In drastically changed circumstances—such as those created by war, enemy occupation, recurring dangers that threaten one's very survival, or simply immersion in situations in which the rules that are accepted seem to be different—it may look as if the old familiar rules do not apply. In such cases, someone can become genuinely convinced that the sort of

---

14. Plato, *Republic,* trans. G. M. A. Grube, rev. C. D. C. Reeve (Indianapolis: Hackett Publishing Co., 1992), Book X, St. 619, 290.

thing that used to be considered morally wrong now is quite acceptable in the changed circumstances.

Because of this, the results of the Milgram experiment probably would not have surprised Plato or Confucius. Both thought that genuinely virtuous people represented a small minority of the population. The vast majority, in their view, would behave well or badly depending on circumstance. In a primitive agricultural society, one important circumstance is whether there is a bad harvest (in which case many people will be close to the edge of survival) or a good one. Confucius' great follower, Mencius (fourth century BCE), remarks that in good years the young men are mostly lazy and in bad years mostly violent.[15]

Threatening or disorienting circumstances represent a greater challenge to a pattern of virtuous behavior than most of us usually have to face. Another kind of challenge is less easy to describe. Sometimes unusual circumstances justify doing something of a sort that normally would be wrong; or maybe not. Cases like this can be difficult to describe, because so many incidental features might turn out to be relevant, and they call for judgment that is keyed to the particular case.

The most familiar example would be the moment when someone who normally never lies or breaks promises might think that, in the present special circumstances, it would be best to lie or break a promise. Telling the truth or remaining silent could hurt someone. So telling a lie can look (this time) like the best option, even if there is a risk that it might undermine the trust in oneself that the person lied to would have.

Immanuel Kant in his old age said that on principle one should never lie, although some commentators have denied that Kant fully held this view.[16] Someone who rejects the view would have to regard the decision of whether to lie as requiring an assessment of relevant factors. How much harm could telling the truth or remaining silent cause? And how much risk of damage to personal relationships might the lie cause? Sometimes this assessment might be fairly easy. But there can be difficult cases. A similar comment applies to any decision that, this time, it might be best not to keep the promise that you made.

A more substantive example is the one provided by the psychologist

---

15. Mencius, trans. D. C. Lau (Harmondsworth: Penguin, 1970) Book VI.A.7, p. 164.

16. Cf. H. J. Paton, "An Alleged Right to Lie: A Problem in Kantian Ethics," *Kant Studien* 45 (1953–4), 190–203.

Lawrence Kohlberg, to illustrate his view of priorities in morality. A man needs a drug to save his dying wife; a pharmacist controls the local supply, and will not accept any reasonable price for the drug. Should the man steal it?

Kohlberg was sure that the answer was "Yes." Let me, for what it is worth, express my view, which is that one needs to know more in order to make an intelligent determination. A great many factors not described by Kohlberg (including a fuller description of what the man's alternatives were or had been) could make a difference in what might be a difficult moral decision. It is especially relevant if whether the man steals the drug would affect whether someone else, who also needs it, could get it.

The point most relevant to the issue of genuine virtue is as follows. Legal scholars often distinguish between "hard cases" and ordinary cases in the law. The former typically involve conflicts or tensions between precedents or accepted principles. Because of these, sometimes no solution will seem obviously, unproblematically right to an unbiased person.

In much this same way, we might distinguish between hard cases and easy cases in morality. Hard cases are ones in which a reasonable solution can be far from evident even to someone who habitually follows established morality. Easy ones are those in which a reasonable solution is readily apparent to anyone who has learned the traditional moral rules. We all know that you should not take the opportunity to kill a neighbor just because he or she is disagreeable. If someone implements the wrong solution in such a case, it is usually assumed that the cause is weakness of will rather than lack of knowledge of what is right.

Hard moral cases may not come up very frequently in the lives of most of us. But how well we perform—or would perform—in them can look like an index of genuine virtue, quite as much as how we would perform in threatening or disorienting circumstances. The insistence running through much of classical Greek and Confucian philosophy is that genuine virtue requires reliably good performance across the range of serious moral decisions. This is a high standard, and it is assumed that most people will not meet it. Part of the standard is good performance in hard cases.

One way in which the role of hard cases emerges is in discussions of what is called the "mean." Finding the mean is a major topic in Book II of Aristotle's *Nicomachean Ethics,* and also the Confucian *Doctrine of the*

*Mean.* One might at first think that this simply concerns moderation. But the point instead is that a range of virtues (courage and generosity are common examples) cannot be reduced to rule-following. Instead they require judgment of the circumstances of each particular case, leading to a determination of what is appropriate in that case.

Courage, for example, is the mean between the extremes of foolhardiness and cowardice. The foolhardy person is always ready to advance into danger and to take risks. The coward always wants not to advance into danger and take risks. Both of these are in this way consistent. The courageous person, on the other hand, will judge in each situation whether what can be gained is worth the risks. If it is, she or he will behave in the situation much like the foolhardy person, advancing into danger. If it is not, she or he will behave much like the coward and withdraw. Similarly, the generous person sometimes, when appropriate, gives money freely like the spendthrift, and sometimes judges that it makes sense to hold on to the money like the miser.

It should be added that, when a great deal is at stake, a judgment of what courage or generosity requires could amount to a moral decision. Aristotle and the Confucians seem to think that the person of ordinary virtuous habits may not be good at making these decisions. More generally, a person of ordinary virtuous habits may not recognize unusual factors in a problematic situation that justify a different sort of choice from the usual one. Rigidity can be a vice, one that paradoxically is a special risk for someone who has very firm habits that involve virtuous behavior in the usual sorts of case.

Two remarks in the *Analects* of Confucius connect with this. Discussing various worthies of old, Confucius says he was different from all of them "in that I have no preconceived notions of what is permissible and what is not."[17] This is normally interpreted as meaning that Confucius is not inflexible, that he thinks it is sometimes important to judge the circumstances of the case. It needs to be emphasized that the flexibility that Confucius claims must not be confused with moral drift. It is abundantly clear that no imaginable circumstances exist in which Confucius would have committed, say, murder, rape, torture, or theft.

Lying and rudeness would be something else. A passage in the *Analects* contains an example of both. A messenger arrived from an unsavory

17. *Analects* Book XVIII.8, 218–9.

person who wished to meet Confucius. Confucius had him told that he was not at home (lying). Then, as the messenger was leaving, Confucius began to play his zithern (a string instrument) and to sing loudly (deliberate rudeness).[18]

The second Confucian remark is the cryptic saying that "The village worthy is the thief of virtue."[19] A standard interpretation of this is provided by Mencius; that the village worthy is motivated too strongly by desire for approval, and hence acts with the wrong attitude. In the condensed Confucian style, it is possible to mean two or more things in the same utterance. Confucius may have been saying also that the village worthy's judgment in hard cases is highly flawed (so that he will self-righteously do something that is rigid and intolerant).

If we accept a standard like that of Plato, Aristotle, or Confucius for genuine virtue, questions remain. The primary manifestation of virtue is in how one behaves. What makes possible the good performance in difficult moral choices? Are certain kinds of training or beliefs especially relevant?

Answers differ. Some include various kinds of knowledge and sensitivity. Aristotle and Confucius both clearly believe that experience of how the world works is highly relevant to good decisions in many kinds of difficult cases. Plato also indicates this, but not so clearly. Confucius also emphasizes an elaborate educational program of refining one's responses and discriminations that has no close parallel in Greek philosophy.

Despite these variations, two factors remain that all three philosophers regard as essential for genuine virtue. One is knowledge of what is most desirable in life. Related to this is a second factor, a commitment to an idea of virtue that implies both emotional involvement and also that virtuous performances will be experienced as satisfying.

All three philosophers share the assumption that genuine virtue must be internalized. The process of becoming a virtuous person is thus a shaping of self, acquiring a second nature in which not to be virtuous would go against the grain. The genuinely virtuous person is thoroughly at home in virtuous behavior, and Aristotle and Confucius both seem to

18. Ibid., Book XVII.20, 208–9.
19. Ibid., Book XVII.13, 205–6.

think that this can be manifested in spontaneous improvisation of virtu-
ous responses to difficult problems. Like any worthwhile skill, this will be a source of enjoyment. Hence
someone acting out of genuine virtue will experience the kind of refined
and especially valued gratification that the psychologist Csikszentmihalyi
found in skilled performances in which one can get caught up. Aristotle
and Confucius (and probably Plato as well) would think that someone
who never enjoys behaving virtuously is not genuinely virtuous.

## A Question About Virtue and Religion

Many people would give a different answer from those given by Plato,
Aristotle, and Confucius to the question of what genuine virtue requires.
This is that genuine virtue requires being religious. A number of issues are
relevant here. What is religion? Does it have an essential component? Are
all religious people alike in some fundamental way? And are all irreligious
people alike in some fundamental way?

These are important questions, and the first especially is highly complicated. But we can begin to investigate them. Bear in mind that this
book is designed to start reflection, not to finish it.

One answer to the first question begins from the fact that a number of
movements have been termed religions, and they do not all have the same
features. For example, most forms of Christianity center on a creed, a set of
beliefs that are implicit in accepting the religion. Judaism and Islam also traditionally center on beliefs that include reference to a supreme being. But
Buddhism also is considered a religion, and it has always been far from obvious whether anything like a creed is central to (or required by) Buddhism.

Buddha's teaching did include a morality, which for example condemned any taking of human or animal life. Most readers will be familiar
with the fact that Christianity and Judaism contain a morality, which goes
back to the Ten Commandments. There is a very comparable morality in
Islam.

It is easy to jump to the conclusion that morality is the total of what
these religions teach about how to live. But this would be a mistake.
Someone could dependably comply with Buddha's morality and still not
be following Buddha's central recommendation; namely, to turn yourself

into someone who has replaced desires with mild preferences, and has a low-key compassion for all living things. Here and there in the *New Testament* there are indications that Jesus' recommendations go well beyond those in moral laws. The Sermon on the Mount advocates purifying your thoughts as well as actions, and a strong recommendation along similar lines is contained in what Jesus says to a rich young man.[20] It can be argued that a change of what you are (as well as moral behavior) is also implicit in Judaism and Islam. Confucianism, despite clear absence of any creed, is occasionally listed as a religion. It too emphasizes the importance of making yourself into a certain kind of person.

This being said, it remains true that the religions familiar to virtually all readers strongly recommend avoiding the obvious forms of immoral behavior. Further, many religions promise rewards that become much less likely if you fail in virtue, and they also threaten punishments to the wicked. All of this seems powerfully motivational. Could someone be genuinely virtuous without all of this?

Before suggesting a line of reply, let me emphasize (yet again) the risks of generalizing. Religious instruction, even if accepted, does not have the same effect on everyone. The ideas about morality held by people who are not religious also can vary greatly.

Besides the risks of generalizing, consider an opposing risk. It is tempting to assume that if nothing is true of all Xs and false of all Ys, then there is no difference between the two groups. But maybe some things are true of more Xs than Ys?

Once we are prepared for these complications, it is easy to see that there is no level of virtuousness that all religious or all irreligious people share. It was widely thought throughout the Middle Ages that some religious people went to hell, and it remains true that someone who by normal standards is religious could repeatedly yield to the worst temptations. On the other side, there were irreligious people in resistance groups during the Nazi occupation of Europe who died painful deaths rather than betray their comrades, and who seemed virtuous in other ways. Presumably thoughts of heaven and hell did not carry any weight with them, but there may have been the thought of whether they could live with themselves after making their decisions.

This still leaves a difficult question: is there a higher correlation between being religious and genuine virtue than between being irreli-

20. *Gospel According to St. Matthew*, 19. 16–26.

gious and genuine virtue? Even if not everyone is alike in each group, might religiousness (or lack of religiousness) be more conducive to genuine virtue? It is a complicated question, requiring, among other things, a clear sense of what is to count as genuine virtue.

There is also a practical difficulty. In order to know who is genuinely virtuous, we would have to know details of people's lives that normally would be hidden. It could amount to spying on people. One might regard something like the Milgram experiment as testing genuine virtue, but the ethical standards for experiments subsequently adopted make it unlikely that such an experiment can be repeated. In practice a great deal remains that we can never know.

Still, there could be relevant evidence. It is worth noting that the two groups in question have been compared in other ways. Michael Argyle reports evidence of a correlation between religious experience and/or prayer on one hand, and self-reported happiness levels on the other.[21] This of course does not mean that all religious people are happy or that no irreligious people are happy, but does point toward factors that appear to make a difference in some cases. One can speculate on whether such factors exist that in some cases can make a difference to genuine virtue. But probably we should not expect definitive psychological evidence any time soon.

## Reflections on Good Impulses and Niceness

Before we return to the main question of this chapter—whether there is a real connection between true virtue and a desirable kind of life—it is worth taking a further look at optimism about the prevalence of human virtue. We have seen that great ancient philosophers were far from sharing this optimism. Even if they are right though, the optimism is not a total delusion. It has roots in what arguably are real features of human life.

One feature, already noted, is that in a prosperous, stable, well-regulated society, very many people will behave reasonably well. Some, from

21. Argyle, *Psychology and Religion. An Introduction* (London: Routledge, 2000), 71. See also 143ff.

Confucius and Plato to Mark Twain and Stanley Milgram, would quickly point out that this is true because tests of virtue do not abound in such a society. Nevertheless, it is hard to shake the sense that all this good behavior does count for something.

Another root of optimism is as follows. It is plausible to view some impulse toward benevolence or sympathy as very widespread among human beings, even if the impulse is most likely to be acted upon when selfish interests are not at stake. The great Confucian philosopher Mencius argued this, as did David Hume.

Mencius' test case was the imagined circumstance in which a small child was crawling toward a well, in which the child would drown. Virtually anyone, he contended, would save the child. Hume's test case involved a man with gout (a painful disease of the feet) walking toward you. Virtually anyone, he contended, would step aside rather than step on the man's feet.[22]

Neither Mencius nor Hume though went so far as to claim that most people are virtuous. The claim was merely that the makings of virtuous behavior were generally present. Our good impulses are not constant. They are more often acted upon when people who need our help or kindness are present to us, or when we are given a description of their situation, than when we might not think of them at all and real thoughtfulness is required. Even if there is an innate tendency to feel benevolent impulses, a large gap lies between this and consistent benevolent behavior.

Benevolence is not quite the same as niceness, although the two often overlap. Many people do seem to be nice most of the time. Perhaps this is because niceness is often not as demanding as benevolence?

It is hard not to be positive about niceness. Most of us greatly prefer to live and work with nice people. Some virtues are associated with niceness, including considerateness and a tendency to meet people halfway. But it is possible to have some virtues and not be (overall) virtuous.

Many of those who kept administering what they thought were serious electric shocks in the Milgram experiment must have been nice people. Many nice people, in order to avoid trouble, went along with Nazi or

---

22. See Mencius Book II.A.6, 82–3; Hume, *Enquiry Concerning the Principles of Morals,* ed. J. B. Schneewind (Indianapolis: Hackett Publishing Co., 1983), 47.

Stalinist authorities. Conversely, there have been virtuous people who were not very nice. Take Socrates for example. He does not appear to have been good at meeting people halfway. His pattern of pursuing philosophical arguments offered a major contribution to human life, but it did involve humiliating unwilling participants in public. It would be widely agreed that the greatness of his virtues much outweighs these social faults. But that does not make him a nice man.

There also is the thought that niceness (while it generally is quite positive) can be a risk factor in high pressure situations. Nechama Tec, in her study of Christians who at great risk saved Jews during the Holocaust, puts first among the common features of the "rescuers" that "They don't blend into their communities."[23] It may be that the agreeable immersion in the community that is part of being a nice person would make it more difficult, in highly threatening conditions, to deviate from the general behavior of the surrounding community than it would be for someone who was more independent and not always so nice.

## Two Sorts of Argument That There Often Can Be a Strong Connection Between Genuine Virtue and the Good Life

We can begin with arguments that stress the inherent psychological rewards of genuine virtue. A first argument is that a genuinely virtuous person's enjoyment of the flow of psychic involvement with the world will make the value of such a person's life at least moderately high, come what may. This argument clearly fits Confucius' and Aristotle's model of genuine virtue, which emphasizes the gratification of virtuous performances. Plato has a separate argument in the *Republic* that lack of genuine virtue entails painful psychological conflicts, whereas the genuinely virtuous person's harmony of mind will be experienced as very rewarding.

In addition, Confucius also argues that one of the rewards of genuine

---

23. Gay Block and M. Drucker, *Rescuers: Portraits of Moral Courage in the Holocaust* (New York: Holmes and Meier, 1992), 6; Nechama Tec, *When Light Pierced the Darkness: Christians' Rescue of Jews in Nazi-Occupied Poland* (New York: Oxford University Press, 1986), 188–89.

virtue is serenity. If the values that flow from genuine virtue are the most important in life, and they come to be within your control, then you have nothing really important to worry about. The average person, who mainly values money, reputation, and sensual pleasures will have a great deal to worry about, because such things are very subject to luck.

These arguments suggest a strong connection between genuine virtue and a desirable life, and indeed this is the view of all three philosophers. The connection is so strong only if they have the truth, and the whole truth, about what genuine virtue is. Let us for the sake of argument assume that there is such a thing as genuine virtue. There still would be two possible ways of dissenting from Confucius', Plato's, and Aristotle's claim of an extremely strong connection between genuine virtue and having a good life. In one view, genuine virtue is quite different from what they think it is; what they describe is not genuine virtue. The other is to hold that there can be more than one kind of genuine virtue, and accordingly there can be genuine virtue whose connectedness with a desirable life is not as strong as it is for the kind extolled by Plato, Aristotle, and Confucius.

Let us look at the idea that what the great ancient philosophers extolled is not genuine virtue. Kant held this view. He thought that genuine virtue would be acting out of a sense of duty as the only possible moral motive. Duty is contrasted with "inclination," personal motives having to do with desire or gratification. It looks as if the gratification in virtuous performances of which Aristotle and Confucius speak, or the appeal of psychic harmony emphasized by Plato, will operate as motives of inclination. Hence they are not moral motives, and do not represent genuine virtue.

This does not mean that Kant thinks it is positively bad to enjoy behaving virtuously. His point is merely that it takes the merit of the performance out of the realm of morality into some different area, connected with merits of a nonmoral sort. Here is one way of seeing his point. Imagine two cases. In the first, you are out walking on a cold day and, in a secluded location, see a man you really dislike drowning. You know that there would be no reward (just more abuse) if you save this person, and no penalties if you simply walk away and think "It couldn't happen to a nicer guy." But you save him. In the second case, you save the person you love most in the entire world.

It looks like you did something very moral in the first case. What about the second case? Do we say, "That was very moral of you, to save the per-

son you love so much"? Hardly. We may think even more strongly that
you are a wonderful person, and we'd be glad that you did what you did.
But whatever credit you get is not *moral* credit.
This example suggests two points. One is that Kant may be right, at
least to a degree, about the nature of morality and moral virtue.
"Morality," like "freedom" and "democracy," is a contestable notion; there
is room for competing ideas of what it includes. Kant may be right about
moral virtue, or he may have part of the truth.

We can continue to think though that some qualities that are not
moral virtues, such as your resourcefulness in saving the person you love,
are nevertheless virtues. We admire them—maybe not in that specific
moral way—and we think more highly of you because of them. If such
qualities are not virtues, then what does the word "virtue" mean?

If virtues exist that are not strictly speaking moral virtues, then
there is no clear reason why there cannot be genuine virtue (of the
sort extolled by the great ancient philosophers) that does not entirely
fit the profile of moral virtue. The profile of moral virtue, if Kant is
right, represents (a) acceptable decisions of the sort that can be judged
by moral standards, that (b) are made out of a motive of duty. What we
can see is that some virtue could satisfy condition (a) even though the
decisions are not made from motives of duty, but rather are made from
appealing motives of a different sort. This could count as virtue (but
of a nonmoral sort) even if we entirely accepted Kant's account of
morality.

Hence the first dissent from the claim that genuine virtue has an
extremely strong connection with a desirable life looks implausible. Even
if one accepts Kant's conception of morality, it looks like there can be
genuine virtue that has this extremely strong connection. What about the
second way?

It seems very hard to deny that there can be genuine virtue, that per-
sists and generally does well on tests of virtue, that does not quite fit the
profile of Plato, Aristotle, and Confucius. If one thinks that the portrayal of
Job in the Bible could be accurate, this would be one example. More generally, we all think we know of people who stubbornly cling to general
rules of morality, interpret these in a sophisticated way, and who do not
seem to derive great satisfaction from their own virtuous performances.
Some of the Germans who defied the Nazis and were killed as a result fit
this profile. If such people are very unlucky, their lives may seem to them

on the whole to be unrewarding even though they have behaved virtuously. Why can't there be more than one kind of genuinely virtuous person?
It seems to me that this question is unanswerable. Genuine virtue cannot be constricted to a single psychological model. If this is true, then the
most that the arguments of Confucius, Plato, and Aristotle give us is that
there *can be* (in some cases) a strong connection between true virtue and
a good life. Because of this, it looks as if the first line of argument merely establishes that—for some kinds of virtuous people (the ones praised in
Greek and Confucian philosophies)—virtue is highly conducive to having a desirable life. There is a connection, but not an entirely general one.

Here is a second sort of argument for a strong connection between genuine virtue and the good life. It suggests a causal connection, so that genuine
virtue makes some important values much more likely. The best presentation
is in the Sermons of Bishop Joseph Butler, an early eighteenth century
philosopher. Butler is concerned first and foremost with undermining the
superficial view that self-interest and altruism are inherently opposed. What
counts as self-interest depends on what you care about. If you care about
other people, you want their well-being. Hence their well-being will contribute to your getting what you want. For the caring person this becomes
a matter of self-interest. If you don't much care for other people, this will
give your interests a narrow, closed quality that is not conducive to happiness. If you do care, there can be more sources of satisfaction.

Hume was influenced by Butler. He also notes advantages to being a
thoroughly reliable person in anything of moral weight; people treat one
better. A "sensible knave" might think, "I'll behave virtuously unless no
one is looking and there would be a big advantage in breaking the rules."
This might work, but Hume contends that the odds are generally against
the sensible knave. People often pick up on the fact that someone is not
to be trusted.

The arguments of Butler and Hume do not claim to show that true
virtue always guarantees a desirable life, or that its lack precludes a life of
some happiness. The claim is rather that we can expect a strong correlation between virtue and the rewards of life. It is not a sure thing, but it is
a very good bet.

Putting the two sorts of argument together, we can see that there are
real connections between virtue and the satisfactoriness of life. In some
cases (the ones that fit Aristotle's and Confucius' models of what is genuine virtue) the connection is very strong. And in general it is statistically

strong. The obvious message is that, even from the point of view of sheer self-interest, virtue is generally a good strategy in life.

## A Final Word About Niceness

Some readers may feel that much of the discussion in this chapter has placed niceness under a cloud. The respects in which someone can be nice without being virtuous, or virtuous without being nice, have been emphasized. Further, it was pointed out that in some major tests of virtue, being nice may make someone more liable to fail.

It is worth saying, as part of a positive "take home" message, that it is possible to be both nice and a virtuous person, and that there are great advantages in this combination. To be a nice person typically contributes to satisfying personal relationships, which can provide many of the rewards of life. The usual advantages of virtue have already been examined.

If there is sometimes a strain between niceness and virtue, it can be largely eliminated by a reflective attitude toward life's problems, and a decision not always to be the same. Niceness typically involves habits of mind of an amiable sort. Part of the argument of this chapter has been that true virtue can require deviating from our habits of mind. In hard cases, we may need to vary our behavior to fit what is appropriate for the situation at hand. It is quite all right to be a nice person. But you need not be nice to people who cause great suffering to others, to those who collaborate with them, or to people who want you to do things that you really shouldn't do.

# Myth Six

# TRUE VIRTUE IS IMPECCABLE

In the last chapter we began to explore the contrast between, on one hand, a record of having followed the traditional moral rules, and genuine or true virtue on the other hand. Philosophers like Plato and Confucius think there is often a large gap between these two things, as Mark Twain suggested in his "The Man That Corrupted Hadleyburg." It seems to emerge as well from the Milgram experiment and from experience in occupied European countries during World War II.

What might we conclude from all of this? One possible response is that none of the evidence matters; that people who are behaving virtuously *now*, under peaceful relatively unpressured conditions, should be considered truly virtuous. This has some immediate plausibility. So many people consistently behave in a virtuous fashion. Why should we not judge that they are virtuous?

There are reasons why it is not easy to maintain. There is a widespread sense that wartime behavior under adverse conditions or the Milgram experiment reveal something that was there all along. It is a shallowness in some people's virtue. That plainly is Plato's and Confucius' view. But it is implicit in our common sense as well, when we speak of "a test of virtue" or "a test of character." The idea is that many of us have not been tested and might not know in advance about how well we would behave under pressure or in disorienting circumstances.

If we accept that unusual circumstances constitute tests of virtue, then it seems implausible to assume that someone who has a record of virtuous behavior in a prosperous and peaceful society is thereby truly virtuous. One obvious alternative is to insist that genuine or true virtue must be able to pass the tests. A person who would, under pressure, collaborate

with the Nazis, or obey the orders of the local tyrants, or administer what
seem to be serious electric shocks to an innocent person, cannot be truly
virtuous. True virtue must be virtue even in very difficult circumstances.
It is a short step from this to the thought that true virtue requires passing
any test; that it must be impeccable.

There is a tension here between two points of view. Each has some
immediate plausibility, but also has problems. Let us call them the Nice
View and the Demanding View. The Nice View holds that people who are
predictably nice to each other and who do not violate any of the major
traditional moral rules meet any reasonable standard for virtue. We might
speculate on how they would behave if a brutal dictatorship gained power,
or if the circumstances of life (and the expectations of how one should
behave) became so disorienting that all of life resembled a Milgram experiment. But this is not our world. In the world as it is, it may seem obvious
that reasonably nice people of the sort described are virtuous.

One of the problems with this is that niceness looks like a set of learned
social mannerisms, which might not connect very well with choices when
a great deal is at stake. Even if we rule out extraordinary circumstances
(e.g., the Milgram experiment or the demands of Nazi occupation authorities), such choices can occur in our lives. Someone who is very nice in
most contexts might decide, for example, to dismiss large numbers of
workers from their jobs when the alternative was a somewhat diminished
profit margin and lessened rewards for top executives. Such decisions are
morally controversial, and it can be argued that whether they are justified
or not depends very much on the case. The immediate point though is that
niceness in most contexts is readily compatible with less-than-nice decisions in matters that deeply affect people's lives.

The general point also remains that true virtue should not be fragile.
Something can be fragile that in fact never breaks because nothing happens to hit it or exert pressure on it. We can easily imagine virtue that, in
a peaceful and prosperous environment, is never really tested, but that
might well become something quite different under even moderate pressure. It is hard to consider this true virtue.

The great problem with the Demanding View is as follows. It is a widely accepted generalization that no human being is perfect. This suggests that,
for any one of us, there will be some test of virtue that she or he would fail.

This leaves two alternatives. One is a concession. It might be said that
true virtue requires being able to pass all tests of virtue, but unfortunately

no human being rises to this level. The other is a modification of the Demanding View. Perhaps whether someone has true virtue or not depends on the severity of the test that would be failed, and also on the person's response afterwards? A classic modification which focuses on the response afterwards is the doctrine, conspicuous in Christianity, that genuine repentance changes a great deal.

This is a preliminary attempt to show that both the Nice View and the Demanding View have specific problems, which may make it unlikely that any simple form of either can be acceptable. A further problem is relevant equally to both views. Both treat virtuousness as a general state: either one is truly virtuous or one is not. (This is complicated by the thought that there can be degrees of virtuousness.) However, considerable psychological evidence suggests that what is normally thought of as virtuousness is not a general state, but rather is usually specific to domains and even to kinds of situation.

This psychological evidence goes back first to a classic study of character.[1] Much further investigation since this work has pointed in the same direction. The cumulative evidence points toward a disunity of the virtues; someone can be, for example, honest but not courageous, or generally very kind to others but not always honest. There also is specificity within a single virtue. Someone can be very honest in money matters, but not in relation to sexual behavior, or very honest in most money matters but not when large corporations or insurance companies are involved.

Many people had recognized these complications and disunities even before the scientific evidence had arrived. Descriptions of people's characters traditionally included judgments such as "is a reasonable person to deal with, except when his authority is challenged," or "is very decent to most people, but can be cruel to family members or other intimates." A widespread traditional idea is that people are sometimes "at their best" and sometimes "at their worst," and that these variations often correlate with the kinds of situation in which they were placed. Someone assigning responsibilities to members of a group could be mindful of this.

Prominent examples show how a general characteristic could function much better in some contexts than in others. Winston Churchill, the great

---

1. Hugh Hartshorne, M. A. May, and F. K. Shuttleworth, *Studies in the Organization of Character* (New York: Macmillan, 1930).

leader of Britain in World War II, was a good case. It was widely recognized that he had a general tendency to be stubborn and unyielding in relation to people whose desires or ideals differed sharply from his. This helped him to be magnificent in his defiance of Hitler, but was less attractive in his dealings with people who had been subject to Britain, such as the Irish or the people of India.

When we talk about "true virtue," we are talking about excellences (and failings) in human behavior. Both psychology and much traditional common sense tell us that the map of human excellences and failings is much more irregular, even for specific individuals, than we might want to believe. We need to consider that map, beginning with the concept of character and the role of character traits in our lives.

## Character Traits

Let us begin with the idea of having a character. Each of us is born with a temperament, a characteristic tonality of emotional responses to the world. One might well remain a cheerful, or a phlegmatic, or an irritable person for one's entire life. But each of these temperaments is compatible with characters ranging from the admirable to the despicable.

Your character is your characteristic way of responding to the world, and specifically to moral problems or problems that have a strong connection with your pursuit of happiness. Your taste in food or in music, or the kinds of things you find funny, typically would not be considered part of your "character." Some things that typically would be considered part of your "character" include the way you behave in deciding whether to keep promises, or whether to hurt people you are tired of, or in attempting (or not attempting) to overcome obstacles to the achievement of personal goals.

In short, character is concerned with three major areas of life. One is that of moral virtue. To have a good character is to be morally virtuous. To have no character is to be morally unreliable. Secondly, there is behavior toward other people whose seriousness does not rise to the level of the moral or immoral. Part of your character is whether you are considerate, or tend to make wounding remarks, or are unreliable in small things. Finally there is the area of life in which some people give up in the face of difficulties, and others exert themselves and keep going. It is often said that encountering and overcoming adversity is good for character, and this means that it strengthens your performance in this area.

Morality and the pursuit of personal projects, and more generally good behavior toward others, sometimes do require a resolute independence of mind and the ability to persevere. Because of this, to have a "strong" character suggests the likelihood of good performances in these areas. To have a "weak" character, conversely, is to be easily influenced and not to persevere in a course of action even when it is very appropriate.

These ideas, which have been a feature of common sense for centuries, offer a way of analyzing what might be required for genuine or true virtue. Plainly true virtue involves strength of character, which when appropriate will produce resistance to pressures, temptations, and disorientation. Further the idea of true virtue implies predictable good performance in relation to the full range of moral problems. Someone who has true virtue will be honest, period—not merely honest in relation to this or that kind of situation—and will predictably display all of the major virtues.

"How can this be?" one might wonder, when both psychological evidence and much of traditional common sense suggest that people generally are more morally reliable in some areas than in others. There is some debate among psychologists as to how much weight situational factors have in individuals' levels of virtuous behavior. Situationists place the greatest emphasis on the situation as the determinant of behavior. Personologists, on the other side, wish to emphasize the characteristic decision pattern of the individual agent.[2] But it is widely agreed that situational factors typically have at least some weight. This makes the idea of true virtue—a high level of virtue across the spectrum of possible virtues —look more like an imaginative ideal than anything that could be a reality.

In short, it looks as if there is a strong case for concession; true virtue is a nice idea, but there isn't any. Someone who adopts this view could agree with the assumption that true virtue is impeccable. But she or he would regard it as conclusively showing that it is an unrealistic idea.

One argument of this chapter runs against this. It suggests that the

---

2. A good account of the debate can be found in David Funder, *Personality Judgment: A Realistic Approach to Person Perception* (San Diego: Academic Press, 1999), Chapter 2; although one needs to bear in mind that Funder himself has been a major figure on the personologist side.

assumption that true virtue is impeccable really is implausible. The argument will appeal to a traditional, widespread idea of true virtue that does not have this implication. Because of this idea, the meaning of "true virtue" would *not* normally be taken to include "without fault." Indeed the normal view is that it is compatible with being human, and having faults and failings.

A second argument shows that when we explore what true virtue might be, we will realize that it is not easy, and may not be entirely common. But it is possible. Further, there have been actual cases. Later in the chapter, as part of this argument, we will look at some cases. First let us continue to examine character traits, and the irregularity of virtuous and faulty elements so often encountered in people's characters.

One sophisticated way of accounting for some of this irregularity is as follows. Much of what makes you the person you are involves general tendencies. An example is the general tendency to be stubborn and unyielding in relation to views and aspirations that simply seem unjustified. As we saw in the case of Winston Churchill, such a general tendency cannot be simply labeled a virtue or simply labeled a vice. In some situations it manifests itself in admirable behavior. In others, it shows up in a way that many people would consider less than admirable.

Much the same is true of an opposite tendency, to attempt to meet uncongenial views halfway in a conciliatory spirit. That certainly did not work with Hitler, as British leaders before Churchill found out. But in other cases (of sorts that occur more often) it can turn out to be intelligent and effective, and would be widely considered decent and virtuous.

This may be part of the basis for the saying of the great seventeenth century French moralist Duc de la Rochefoucauld that treats virtues and vices as interwoven:

> "Vices have a place in the composition of virtues just as poisons in
> those of medicines; prudence blends and tempers them, utilizing
> them against the ills of life."[3]

Being generally stubborn and unyielding in relation to opposing views might be thought of as a vice (although I suggest that whether it is or not

---

3. Francois, Duc de la Rochefoucauld, *Maxims,* trans. L. W. Tancock (Baltimore: Penguin, 1959), Maxim 182, 57.

depends on the case), and la Rochefoucauld suggests that it can still play a part in virtue (as it did in the admirable virtue of Winston Churchill).

However one speaks of the general tendency, the crucial point is as follows. What matters most is a sense of when it is appropriate to act on that tendency, and when it is better to modify it. This has to be part of what la Rochefoucauld has in mind when he speaks of "prudence," which blends and tempers what (normally) are virtues and vices.

At least one translator (Arthur Waley) has taken Confucius to be making a similar point. Virtues and faults "belong to a set."[4] The thought seems to be that the two are interwoven, and that one might be able to predict someone's virtues from her or his faults.

Confucius, who has been widely taken as an example of true virtue, repeatedly made it clear that he was not perfect. This realization required, as he saw it, a special willingness to be open to criticism, and more generally to learn from other people. He is described as being entirely free of arbitrariness, inflexibility, rigidity, and selfishness.[5]

The image of true virtue that emerges in Confucius' account is something like this. You begin with a general disposition (cooperative and conscientious) that points in the right direction. This then becomes refined in an education of the emotions (in which ideas gained from the classics, interactions with others of a ritual sort, and also music play a part). This process promotes a fine-grained responsiveness to particular situations.

Because of human fallibility, self-corrective tendencies remain crucial. The self-correction requires two elements. One is that you care about it: you want to get things right. This contributes to a second aspect, the ability to pick up cues from other people that perhaps, this time, what you did was faulty. The openness to criticism does not mean, of course, that if people thought what you did was wrong they necessarily were right. (The moral views of the people around you could be generally faulty.) It does mean that you will consider other people's views, and take them seriously.

We can see here an image of true virtue that incorporates the reality of human fallibility. Part of the virtue is in how you respond to your own fallibility. Something a little like this emerges in Aristotle's suggestion that,

---

4. *Analects,* trans. Arthur Waley, (New York: Vintage Books, 1938), Book IV.7, 103.

5. *Analects,* trans. Edward Slingerland (Indianapolis: Hackett Publishing Co., 2003), Book IX.4, 87.

when you are searching for a proper course of action that lies between two extremes, one factor to be considered is your own possible one-sidedness. If anything, he suggests, you should lean a little toward the extreme that lies further from your own instinctive tendencies.[6] Indeed the thought that a virtuous person responds to actual or possible mistakes in a special way is widespread. We have already noted the religious idea of repentance as an example. Even in nonreligious contexts, we tend to think more highly of the virtue of someone who really is bothered by her or his faulty behavior and takes steps to correct the tendencies that led to it.

All of this helps in understanding how true virtue can be compatible with human fallibility. Someone like Confucius, who emphasized his fallibility, can be thought to be truly virtuous. Plainly the fact that the lapses are not extremely serious does matter; someone who just occasionally committed a murder would not be thought truly virtuous. But the attitude to virtue as an ongoing process also matters. We are more likely to consider someone virtuous who takes the process seriously, and as a result engages in self-correcting behavior.

All of this leads us back to the idea of character, and of what it is to have a good character. It is tempting to take character simply as a sort of descriptive summary of a person's tendencies in key areas of life (those of morality, more broadly the treatment of others, and of the pursuit of happiness). But a collection of psychological processes of self-control appear strongly associated with strong and good character. These include processes of self-monitoring, asking yourself hard questions about what you are doing, being open to other people's criticisms, reminding yourself of general principles that you tend to accept, and constraining yourself from violations of these principles. Arguably these also can include the possibility that, in *this* unusual situation, something different from your normal behavior is called for.

This aspect of character includes psychological forces. They are an important part of some people's lives. But there also are people in whose lives they do not play any conspicuous part. Bearing all of this in mind, we can answer the question of how it can be that there could be genuinely virtuous people, despite the situational elements in normal human

---

6. Aristotle, *Nicomachean Ethics,* trans. Terence Irwin, Second Edition (Indianapolis: Hackett Publishing Co., 1999), 1109b, 29.

behavior. The answer does not require human perfection. It does require a strong, ongoing presence of self-monitoring and self-constraint of the sort described, in which situational lapses can be curtailed, modified, and reconsidered.

## The Assertion of Character in the Swirl of Life

It may be useful to view the problem of genuine virtue in a broader context. This will include general facts of human life. It also will include two dilemmas, one social and the other personal, that attend these facts.

One general fact is that no one, not even someone who is unusually serious and moralistic, can make all significant choices in a reflective way. Some courses of action involve a dense chain of choices (at various points you could change direction or modify your stance), and it will be impossible to pause for each one. Many moral choices are presented suddenly and require immediate decision, so that even to take time to reflect is to make a choice.

Because of this, even highly intelligent people who really would like to be virtuous will make many of the important moral choices in their lives reactively. They will rely on habit, or on inhibition ("I could not bring myself to do that sort of thing"), or on a quick reading of a familiar moral rule or policy. Much of moral virtue, like good driving, is a matter of having good reactions when there is not much time to think.

Moral rules often take the form of "Thou shalt" or "Thou shalt not," which suggests that there will be no exceptions. An increased tendency in recent centuries suggests that at least some moral rules do have imaginable exceptions. For example, someone who in general thinks that lying is wrong might hold that there are occasions when it is actually the decent choice. If the main effect of a lie is to spare an innocent person's feelings, that could be relevant. Similarly, there are cases in which we wouldn't expect someone to keep a promise.

One way of accommodating this is to speak, as the philosopher W. D. Ross did, of certain things as being *prima facie* wrong. That is, at first glance they can look wrong; but then one can take other factors of the situation into account. These might include the risk of badly hurt feelings, of other forms of collateral damage from telling the truth or keeping the promise, and the likelihood of missed opportunities of a major sort. When these are reflectively considered, the judgment can veer from "Do not do" to "Do."

Another way of accommodating the sense of possible exceptions is to distinguish between, on one hand, things that never should be done in any imaginable situation (e.g., torturing an innocent person) and, on the other, things that should not be done lightly. We could speak of someone as having a policy of, say, not lightly breaking a promise. A policy, unlike a rule, does not require doing the same sort of thing in every case. To have a policy is then to have to make judgment calls, such as whether these peculiar circumstances justify doing the sort of thing that normally you never would do.

Someone who thinks that some moral rules have imaginable exceptions is highly unlikely to pause frequently to consider whether—right now—one is confronted with an exception to the familiar rule. For one thing, a stance of looking for exceptions is bound to undermine loyalty to the policy of usually following the rule. Beyond this, there is the practical difficulty of taking all that time, again and again. Further, in ordinary cases it should be evident that there are not likely to be special factors that justify an exception to the rule.

Consequently, even someone who believes that familiar moral rules have exceptions that call for reflective judgment is virtually certain to make the vast majority of moral choices quickly, acting out of habit or along the lines of what a general policy dictates for ordinary cases. Reflective pauses will occur mainly when something looks unusual, suggesting special reasons for doing what you normally would not do.

This reliance most of the time on habits, general rules, or policies imparts a steadiness to behavior. It increases the chances that most people will continue to behave much as they have, as long as there is not a drastic change in the general environment. It promotes moral stability.

A second general fact about human life points in the opposite direction. People do change. Virtually everyone changes significantly in the course of her or his life, not only in looks and in tastes, but also in the kinds of behavior one could expect. Habits and moral policies may lessen the rate of change, making it usually very gradual. But over a period of decades, the cumulative change is likely to be significant. Further, if there are sharp changes in someone's personal situation (e.g., marriage, divorce, immigration, loss of a job, involvement in a war), the change might be not so gradual. This is also true if the general social surround changes drasti-cally: if, say, there is occupation by a foreign power, or a civil war, or a "cultural revolution" of sorts.

The facts of personal change amount to a social dilemma, and also a personal dilemma for each of us. The social dilemma is as follows. A stable and secure society requires that we be able to count on most of the people around us to behave—and to continue behaving—along the lines of understood moral policies. This requires the leverage of hold-ing people responsible for their actions. It is widely known that, if you do something very wrong, you can be blamed or punished for it, even years later.

Years later, however, you may be a very different sort of person. Most of us do not change drastically over, say, five or ten years. Over thirty or forty years, though, a much larger number of us will have become very different. There certainly are cases in which someone who, in her or his youth, had been a cold-blooded killer, seems genuinely to have become an upstanding and caring person. We want to hold people responsible for their actions, but in some of these cases it seems awkward and uncom-fortable. If so-and-so, who is about to be punished for those awful things he did thirty or forty years ago, really seems to have become a very dif-ferent person, we usually do not know what to say. In a way, we would rather not think about it. It is simpler to think of people as always being the same, and to go on with our normal practices of punishment. (And, if we forgave some people who seemed really to have greatly changed, we might worry that this opened the door to all sorts of playacting and trickery.)

The social order does generally require judgments of responsibility, which help to deter antisocial behavior. Because we would like it all to make sense, there is a general tendency to want, and to insist on, enough stability in people's natures to justify these judgments.

This is part of what we want. But, on the other hand, the world changes; if there is not some adaptive change in people over time, there can be real risks of cultural and social stagnation. So most of us want peo-ple not to be too unchanging. Not very many people would like to have a population of Victorians in the twenty-first century. The two social needs here—to have enough stability to anchor a sense of responsibility, and to have enough change to avoid stagnation—seem to pull in oppo-site directions.

Something like this is true on a personal level as well. The man or woman who simply stays the same can over time come to resemble a fossil. On the other hand, someone who seems like a different person every few months may lack much sense of an ongoing meaning or coherence in her or his life. Such a person also is unlikely to enjoy the satisfactions of long-term continuing personal relationships. Again, there is an obvious need for stability and continuity, and also an obvious need for change.

It is not easy to reconcile all of these needs. But one obvious thought is that the societal and personal needs for stability especially concern moral decisions, major life choices of other sorts, and close personal relations. A degree of stability and continuity in these areas could be compatible with a significant degree of change, as it were, around the edges. The phrase "around the edges" can be taken to refer to qualifications (rather than downright reversals) of a person's moral policies, and to real changes in various features of everyday life and personal relations that do not amount to major life choices.

This brings us back yet again to character. Plainly people's characters do change; it would be odd and unfortunate if a person's character did not change at all over, say, thirty or forty years. But some change is compatible with a high degree of stability in general moral commitments, and with continuity in other major aspects of life.

Given this stability, someone can exert the processes of self-control that lie at the heart of character in order to keep up general moral commitments. This will require more work in some areas of choice than in others. In the light of the degree of truth in situationist psychology, such a person will have to be alert to (and to cope with) outright blindspots, and more generally areas of life in which her or his normal instinctive responses are often wanting. If this sort of self-correction is pursued on an ongoing basis and is conducted well, there is no clear reason why it could not result in genuine virtue.

This makes genuine virtue seem, at least in the abstract, possible. But there is nothing to suggest that it will be easy. There are two sources of difficulty.

One is that, as it has just been portrayed, this process requires a certain amount of reflection and effort. Intermittently it will be strenuous. It also has the disadvantage of undermining the rosy view of ourselves that most of us like to have. It is tempting to see yourself as the heroine or hero in a movie of your life. But perhaps no one is always heroic, or lovable, or admirable. The self-monitoring and self-constraint that I have suggested is required for genuine virtue will not make self-approval impossible. But it will qualify it, and thus diminish what might seem like an innocent pleasure. All in all, it will represent a kind of psychological exercise that needs to be carried on when you probably don't feel like doing it.

This portrait of corrective processes as aids to virtue should be enlarged. Self-monitoring and self-criticism often play a part. But so do comments from others, especially friends. There are many differences between a real friend and a mere "buddy," including depth of concern and commitment. Arguably one difference is that a friend who really cares for you, can say, "Why did you do that?" or "Do you really want to. . . ?" in a helpful way that provokes reflection and corrective tendencies. Such friendly criticism can be invaluable, but requires tact on the part of the friend and a willingness to listen on the part of the person being criticized.

The second source of difficulty is as follows. Judgment is required, both in determining what you should make yourself do and in determining the occasions and direction of self-monitoring and self-approval. Self-criticism can be overdone. It can be excessive or too frequent (or both). Furthermore, a good deal of self-monitoring of decisions in which not much is at stake, or of trivial personal interactions, can lead to excessive self-consciousness. In much of everyday life one should simply do what comes, and be prepared to live cheerfully with an imperfect result.

Determining what you should do can be very difficult if the world is changing (as it always is), so that there is room for doubt as to whether the sort of thing that used to be done is always still appropriate. It is possible to be too strict and too rigid. Famous Roman examples include Cato the elder and Cato the younger; both were masters of rectitude, with very little that was situational in their behavior. This could be highly admirable, especially when it involved taking a stand against political corruption or against the general air of decadence that was beginning to pervade their society. But it also could be arrogant and lacking in human sympathy, as traditional rules were rigidly applied.

While the most familiar kinds of moral decisions usually are clear-cut for anyone with a goodwill, we have seen that there can be unusual cases in which this is not true. Special factors, or changes in the world, can complicate the picture. In the end, no reliable road map or rational procedure will provide good decisions in all of these hard cases.

We might reasonably think that someone who is genuinely virtuous ought to be good at making these difficult moral decisions. But this need not entail a perfect record. It is especially important to keep this in mind in relation to people who, because they have considerable power and responsibility (e.g., presidents or military leaders), or merely because they live in difficult circumstances full of turmoil, are constantly making moral decisions in hard cases. We might be impressed if, given hindsight, we see that they usually got it right.

The attitude of these people to their own questionable decisions also can affect our estimate of such people. In some cases brooding over something that might have been a poor decision is merely self-destructive. But often there is continuing involvement with whoever suffered from it. A genuinely virtuous person who had made a questionable decision might well make some effort to mitigate the consequences, or "to try to make things right."

There also is the possibility of learning from mistakes. A very nice dramatization of this appears in a work of fiction, *The Red Badge of Courage* by Stephen Crane, set in the American Civil War. The young protagonist, put into battle, gets the business of courage wrong. The next time, he gets it right.

It is always tempting to see genuine virtue as something that would have to characterize a lifetime, as opposed to some minutes in a life; and at a certain point we do tend to assume that it will be permanent. But obviously people do not spring from their mothers' wombs as genuinely virtuous. There has to be a learning process; part of this inevitably will involve moral decisions, made by someone who is still inexperienced and who may be under pressure.

This process requires a balance. On one hand, someone who is on her or his way to genuine virtue should not be indifferent to faulty moral decisions. But on the other hand it is undesirable to be paralyzed by moral regret. The appropriate view should be long-term, extending forward through a lifetime. Lapses can register, as objects of regret but also as lessons learned. Any regret can be tempered by a resolve to do better.

## Cases of Genuine Virtue

We have not speculated as to what percentage of the population would qualify as genuinely virtuous. It is clear that Plato and Confucius both thought that it would not be a large number. This did not mean they thought the great majority of people were evil or bad. Very probably both of them thought only small numbers of people were what we would call evil. The vast majority of the population appears, in their views, to be in the middle zone between genuine virtue and evil, their behavior depending very much on the situations they are placed in.

Perhaps this underestimates the incidence of genuine virtue in the world? There may well be, and have been, sizable numbers of cases. One difficulty in documenting most of these is the lack of detailed information about people's lives.

Occasionally a detailed portrayal is available. Some readers will immediately think of the lives of saints. Let me return to two lives of philosophers: Confucius and Socrates.

The life of Confucius is portrayed in the *Analects* of Confucius, compiled by his students and their students in the generations after his death (c. 475 BCE). Plainly it is an admiring portrait, but part of what comes through is a man who was repeatedly concerned with his fallibility and the need for self-improvement. A characteristic quotation is this:

"The Master said, 'Do I possess wisdom? No, I do not.'"

But he goes on to say that if even a simple peasant asks a question, he will work it out with him.[7]

It looks clear that Confucius thought that he had made some choices, in his interactions with others, in a less than perfect way; although the details of which these might have been remain obscure. (Indeed who can live, for any considerable period of time, without making some such choices in a less than perfect way?) Certainly he felt justified, at least at the time, in violating some rules of behavior that he normally would have

---

7. *Analects,* trans. Slingerland, Book IX.8, p. 89. Confucius' denial that he was wise should be put in the context of what I have claimed is a paradox of wisdom: if you think you are wise, then you very likely are not. See my "Morality, Ethics, and Wisdom," in *Handbook of Wisdom: Psychological Perspectives,* eds., Robert Sternberg and Jennifer Jordan (Cambridge: Cambridge University Press, 2005), 245–71.

followed. Remember the incident, mentioned in Chapter 5, in which he deliberately lied and was rude. But it is likely that he simply thought that these were justified exceptions to the general rule, given the circumstances. Socrates is portrayed in a number of dialogues by Plato and also in the *Memorabilia* of Xenophon. Xenophon was not a philosopher but a military leader, one of whose exploits involved the escape of a group of Greeks (who had fought on the losing side of a civil war in Persia) through the Persian Empire back to Greece. In both accounts Socrates appears highly admirable.

Was he without fault? Plato and Xenophon may have thought so. Aspects of Socrates' life come through that may strike many modern readers as less than perfect. Like some more recent figures that came to represent a high degree of moral perfection (e.g., Mahatma Gandhi, Leo Tolstoy), Socrates' relations with immediate family may have been less exemplary than those with the wider world. The philosophical interrogation that was his trademark must have been enormously beneficial for some, and made a huge contribution to human history. But sometimes it looks like bullying. Whether it was must remain debatable, but one could consistently hold (1) that Socrates was a truly virtuous person, and (2) that on some occasions (perhaps with his wife Xantippe, and arguably with some people who simply did not want to think philosophically) he did not behave well.

These two cases provide examples of what qualifies as true virtue by any normal standard, even though it was not impeccable. Confucius explicitly was very open to a view of his life as not impeccable, and a balanced view of Socrates would not regard his life as impeccable. There is every reason to suppose that there have been, and are, many lives that would qualify as truly virtuous, but not impeccable. In many of these, reflective, self-corrective tendencies would play a major role.

## Conclusion

In philosophy a new insight often leads to a new confusion. It is quite possible that most people who have always lived in a secure and prosperous society simply equate virtue with a record of virtuous behavior. That there can be a gap between them—one that can become evident in dramatic ways—will be for them a new insight. The Milgram experiment shocked and disturbed many people and gave rise to this new insight. For those who had read Plato's *Republic* or the *Analects* of Confucius, it was an old insight, but even for many of them the Milgram dramatizations must have been unsettling.

The desire to think simply is a persistent and widespread human desire. One simple thought is that people who seem virtuous in their daily life are virtuous. When people like that administer what they think are dangerous electrical shocks in a psychological experiment, or when one imagines them with Plato's ring of invisibility, that simple thought looks untenable. The next simple thought is that what is required for true virtue is not merely virtuous behavior under present circumstances, but rather virtuous behavior in any conceivable circumstances.

This is very much like the insistence of the seventeenth century philosopher René Descartes, responding to increased awareness of possibilities of error, that true knowledge requires no possibility of error at all. It has been widely objected that this sets the standard for knowledge artificially high. The standard in ordinary use is not quite so high. We can get things right and have knowledge, given a strong basis for what we believe, even if our basis has allowed a very slight outside chance of error.

In much this way, the idea of true virtue in traditional common sense does require that someone be able generally to pass tests of virtue more difficult than many people encounter in their lives, but it does not require perfection. True virtue is not impeccable. If the concept of true virtue did require perfection, it might be largely useless (except as an abstraction).

Despite our urge for simplicity of thought, traditional common sense in this area allows for complications. Many of these concern virtue as an ongoing process, which includes the learning curve of becoming virtuous and of stabilizing a degree of virtue. There is no reason to assume that the learning curve will reach up to perfection, that there will be a point after which there will never be subpar behavior.

True virtue requires not merely a good record (or the likelihood of one) in difficult cases. It also requires a complex set of attitudes to choices that turn out to be less than good. These include a degree of regret (especially if the mistake or lapse is of a fairly serious nature), a sense of responsibility to any injured parties, and an ongoing process of self-monitoring and self-criticism to limit poor choices. Dramatic recognition of much of this occurs throughout Western literature. Some readers will think of the *Confessions* of St. Augustine. In some ways the most probing examination is contained in the *Analects* of Confucius.

Finally, moderation in self-criticism is entirely consistent with virtue. To disregard or ignore serious moral lapses, especially when other people are hurt, is irresponsible and feckless. But to dwell on them can be—depending on the case—unreasonable and counterproductive. To dwell on small lapses would be to rob life of its spontaneity.

# How Can We Know
# What Has Value?

Not easily. Part of the argument of this final chapter will be that often we cannot attain a basis for judgments of value that would meet the standards for knowledge. Many judgments will be little more than guesswork, conjecture, or opinion. Occasionally there is a favorable conjunction of two factors that are required for knowledge in this area. One is that the person who evaluates is in a good position to know the nature of that of which she or he judges the value. The other is a strong preparation for making sound judgments of value.

By value I will continue to mean how good or not good something is in the context in which it occurs, apart from to what it leads (i.e., apart from its causal effects). This is to contrast what is desirable in its context, for itself (which is the subject of this chapter), with what is good as a means. Money is a means to a variety of things; but merely having money, apart from these causal effects, is a negligible factor in anyone's life. Conversely, a set of experiences, a way of life, or a relationship can play a role in a life that (apart from whatever are its causal effects) contributes to that life being better or worse.

Our present concern lies in ways in which we can know about how good or bad something is in its context. How can we come to make assured judgments about what is important in life, even apart from its causal effects? What makes the difference between knowing and merely having an opinion?

A loose analogy may help to make this clearer.[1] Many judgments that

---

1. There are a number of reasons, which will emerge in our discussion, why this analogy is loose rather than very close. One is discussed in the Appendix, Number 11.

an event happened in a certain way amount merely to opinion. The suggestion is that most value judgments also amount merely to opinion. What is required for a judgment of value to be more than a mere opinion (and to amount to knowledge)? Perhaps it is elements like those required for Bloggs' opinion that, say, Blech shot Smurf to amount to knowledge.[2]

On most accounts, for Bloggs to know that Blech shot Smurf (as opposed to merely having an opinion that that's what happened), at least three things must be the case. First, "Blech shot Smurf" has to be a correct statement. You cannot know something if it isn't correct. Secondly, it is normally required that Bloggs be confident that Blech shot Smurf. If he presents it as an offhand guess, then it is not knowledge.[3]

Thirdly, he is entitled to be confident. This is a matter of being in a good position to judge, and of having really good grounds for what he says. Position can count for a great deal. If Bloggs was no more than ten feet away from Blech and Smurf and had a clear view, then (especially if he also has good eyesight) it looks like he is in a good position to be confident of what he says. In any ordinary case—especially one in which there were no large problems of interpretation—we would say that this amounts to his having really good grounds for what he says.

Suppose though that there were extraordinary deceptive circumstances, such as a hypnotist engaged in getting Bloggs to believe that Blech was shooting Smurf. (Meanwhile, independent of the hypnotist's activities, Blech really does shoot Smurf.) Genuinely good grounds for judgment have to be such as to overcome whatever are the obstacles to knowledge, and not to be based on coincidences. In the freakish case just described, this requires that Bloggs' belief not be controlled by the

---

2. In putative cases of ethical knowledge, the element of personal commitment (explored in the Appendix, Number 11) also, in my view, will be required.

3. This generalization has exceptions. Sometimes when someone comes up with the correct information, we are able (on the basis of what that person had been exposed to) to say, "You knew it all along." Bloggs may think that his saying, "Maybe 1492 was the date on which Columbus arrived in America" was a guess, but if he had been told this repeatedly we can think that it is more than a guess. Similarly we sometimes say that someone knows something, at some level, but the knowledge is "repressed." It might take hypnosis for Bloggs to be able to articulate his having seen Blech shoot Smurf. Normally however, a guess is a guess, and we judge that real knowledge requires confidence as well as the grounds for confidence.

hypnotist. Bloggs must have a belief that is caused by the correctness of what he believes (and not simply caused by something else).

In roughly this way, if Bloggs knows that something has value (or has no value, or negative value) then (1) what he believes must be right, and (2) he must be confident of his belief. Also (3) he must be in a good position to be confident of his value judgment, having really good grounds. His belief must be caused by the correctness of what he believes.

Can any judgment of value pass this test? And if so, how? What could be the counterpart of being ten feet away from Blech and Smurf (when Blech shot Smurf), and having good eyesight and a clear view?

# Being in a Position to Judge the Value of Something

There may be more than one way to be in a position to judge the value of something.[4] The most obvious one is to experience it. Suppose that one said that such-and-such is really wonderful, or really awful, and someone asks, "What makes you think so?" or "How do you know?" An effective reply is "Because I have experienced it."

We might say this about forms of life we had entered into, about social settings, or about particular experiences or interactions. Thus someone might say "I know how awful it is to spend long hours at repetitive tasks on an assembly line, and to come home extremely tired every day." Or it might be "I know how awful it is to live in a society in which there are many things that simply cannot be said, and the secret police are everywhere." Someone can say, "To be in love with a fine person who loves you back is wonderful; I know because I have experienced it." All of these statements are idiomatic, ordinary things to say, reflecting assumptions in our ordinary discourse about how we come to know about what has or lacks value.

Two points emerge immediately from this pattern. One is as follows. A theme in this book suggests that desire, which John Stuart Mill had

---

4. One possible objection to the line of argument of this chapter is that it fails to distinguish between what simply has value (from a neutral point of view) and what has value for some specific person. This is considered in the Appendix, Number 12.

nominated as the sense of value and which has a powerful influence on our goals and aspirations, is on the whole a very unreliable indicator of value. Most of the things that we desire are ones that we have not ourselves experienced. A few are: some desires can be to retain what we already have had, or to have more of what had seemed wonderful. But very many desires are simply for what seems alluring or "pushes our buttons," and when experienced may or may not seem valuable. Folk wisdom recognizes this. A common saying reports the special danger (in many cases) of actually getting what one wants.

Secondly, it should be obvious that, even if we have experienced something and even if we can assume that we have some appropriate sense of the value of what was experienced, we have to be cautious about generalizing from this. Someone else's experience of work on the assembly line may be very different from ours. Bloggs was bored out of his skull. But Smith organized in her mind various problems that could be thought about, or experiences that could be relived, and it was not bad for her. There are stories of extremely disciplined people confined in horrific circumstances who somehow managed to inject positive elements into the experience.

Similarly, not all experiences of love relations will be the same. It is debatable whether anyone can have a genuinely positive experience of life in a police state. But some people's interests will be less vulnerable than others' to intrusion, and the constraint or awfulness can vary considerably.

Thus what you know may be at most the value (or lack of value) of what you experienced. This could suggest what the likely value (or lack of value) is or was for others as well, but there is a difference between suggestiveness and assured knowledge. In some cases, perhaps, observation of others may strongly suggest that the pattern holds; what was wonderful (or awful) for you was pretty generally wonderful (or awful) for them. Might this amount to knowledge of the value of what they experienced? This is a difficult question that does not admit of a general answer. The degree to which we have knowledge, or something approaching knowledge, of other people's lives and experiences varies enormously.

Here is a generalization that does apply to any area of thought and opinion in which we might be inclined to speak of knowledge. There generally will be a wide gray area between, on one hand, opinion that has hardly any basis at all and on the other hand, what counts as knowledge. Some opinions have fairly good grounds, but we might judge that the grounds are not quite strong enough to allow us to say that they amount to knowledge. Hence opinions that do not come to the standard of knowledge are not all to be disdained. They may represent genuine insight and likely truths.

This can be true even for opinions generated by desire. In some cases, perhaps, desire is an intimation of something important, even if it does not by itself confer knowledge. We might learn from what we desire that some things, if experienced, could be important (in a positive way) for us. This is compatible with a degree of wariness about too quickly assuming that what is desired will be wonderful in actual experience.

Are there other ways to be in a good position to judge the value of something without actually experiencing it? In nonethical forms of knowledge, a standard route to knowledge is via the testimony of someone else who is a reliable authority. Suppose that Bloggs had a clear view of Blech's shooting Smurf and has good eyesight, and furthermore is a dependably truthful person. If he tells you that Blech shot Smurf, under normal circumstances you can reasonably claim to know it. Similarly you usually can claim to know facts that you read in a reliable encyclopedia (if you read carefully), and in much this way it is possible to know truths in mathematics that you are personally unable to prove.

If wise people exist who are reliable judges of what is right, then perhaps (as Aristotle suggested) we can know what is right on the basis of their testimony. Similarly we might perhaps know what has value on the basis of the testimony of reliable judges of value. Can we be sure who are the reliable judges? Some people may seem unusually judicious, with experience of a large variety of social phenomena. This would certainly seem to increase the likelihood that their judgments are reliable. But in order to *know* this, we might have to be wise ourselves.

A more plausible substitute for personal experience could be as follows. Even if we have not had anything like a certain kind of set of experiences, we might know someone well who has. Close and empathetic observation might then give us a sense that such-and-such is a wonderful (or awful, or something in between) way to live, or a wonderful (or awful) set of circumstances. A very good biography might give us something similar.

But in both cases there is the thought that neither the biographer nor we will have seen everything. Significant features of someone's life could be shielded from view, and that would change one's sense of the value of portions of that life. Even friends and biographers may have little idea of some of the peculiarities of Bloggs' life.

Consider another possible substitute for personal experience. After reading a novel, or seeing a film or play, we often have the sense of glimpsing a world of experience that is largely new to us. You can feel that you have learned something about life. In fact a great deal of what most people think they know about life has been shaped, or simply provided, by films, novels, and plays. Why cannot this vicarious experience, like actual lived experience, put us in a position to make appropriate judgments of value?

Arguably it can. The difficulty is in knowing how trustworthy, in terms of realism, the source of vicarious experience is. There are two ways in which we might worry about how trustworthy the source of a particular view of human life is. One is that it might turn out that it presents something unusual as if it is actually the norm. Films often offer appealing visions of cases in which ill-prepared, careless people somehow get everything they want. No doubt this sometimes does happen in real life. Human life is not a simple sort of mechanical system; odd and unlikely things do happen. There is no reason why a film, novel, or play could not represent one of these. The representations though become treacherous if they subtly downplay the fact that what they represent is odd and unlikely.

The other worry is as follows. Any deceptiveness (in terms of values in experience) is multiplied if everything that is gritty, messy, unpleasant or disappointing is either sweetened or eliminated from the picture. In anything real that extends beyond a brief episode—even in the most wonderful and really lucky sets of experiences—there always will be bits that are gritty, messy, unpleasant, or disappointing. Best-case scenarios, over time, will never be absolutely perfect. To provide silver linings without realistic clouds is deceptive. It is dangerously deceptive to portray cases in which everything always works easily and beautifully, without glitches and flaws. This discourages the virtues of patience, resilience, and readiness for a degree of accommodation. To adapt an ancient Persian saying, soft popular entertainment can breed soft people.

Often a film or novel can offer a mixture of the revelatory and the deceptive. A nice example is provided in Andrei Makine's fine novel, *Once Upon the River Love*. Youths growing up in Siberia in the Soviet era suddenly are given a vision of lives of great freedom and excitement in a Jean Paul Belmondo film, which they view again and again. Most of us would agree that there was something true in what they saw, about greater freedom and more opportunity in the West for personal design of paths of enjoyment. But there also was something highly unrealistic, as usual in escapist films. In the novel, the young men discover this when they finally get to the West.

Escapist films and other deceptions usually are harmless in most settings. Many of us go to movies more for release than for a taste of reality. Mature people of some experience will not be deceived in any case. Inexperienced viewers, on the other hand, may be influenced, and can make important decisions about their lives on the basis of a wishful view of the possibilities. Perhaps some of this is inevitable; wishful thinking is not uncommon, and there may be a basic human urge to simplify and to ignore difficulties.

Some novels, films, and plays can be revelatory through and through, giving a sense of a likely reality of experiences or states of being that might be alien to most of us. This is particularly possible in novels, which allow for an accumulation of detail and indicated shadings. In plays and films, good acting can sometimes suggest the complexity that a novel might create at greater length. One example in my experience was a beautifully acted English production (with Robert Stephens) of *King Lear,* which managed (among other things) to recreate well the mental world of someone who was old, displaced, and confused. It reportedly was much admired by psychiatrists. Novels can recreate mental worlds, and at the same time place them in a discursive framework. This is true of the two great eighteenth century novels, Voltaire's *Candide* and Johnson's *Rasselas,* which address the central topic of this book, the good life. Chapter 25 in *Candide* seems especially good in recreating the insipid quality that life would have for someone who can readily get everything that he or she wants.

In cases such as this, the novel, play, or film leaves the thought, "Yes, it could very well be like this." We can have the sense of having learned something important about life as it might be. In a way this is puzzling, because when people try to *say* what they have learned, it often sounds banal. One suggestion has been that novels, plays, and films model what might be realities of human life. A model has the function of enabling us to see more clearly features that, in the crowded and hard-to-take-in world of reality, would normally be hard to see clearly.[5]

Let me summarize what we have just been exploring. Normally the best

5. See Ira Newman, "Fiction and Discovery," Ph.D. diss., University of Connecticut, 1984.

way of being in a position to make a judgment of value is to have experienced what is to be evaluated. This presents drawbacks and risks, though. The chief risk is in generalizing about the value of experiences, some of which will be in subtle ways importantly different from one's own.

A secondary way of being in a position to make a judgment of value is to rely on the testimony of wise people. This can carry you some distance, although there always may be a risk that your authorities are not so wise after all. Another way is to observe people closely and empathetically. Yet another is to have learned about features in life from literature or film. Both of these have risks. Close observation may not be close enough, in that people often shield key features of their lived experience from others. The literary or cinematic sources of much of our sense of what life is like may be more tainted or one-sided than we think they are.

The substitutes for personal experience, in short, are often better than nothing, and sometimes are really satisfactory. But they have to be treated with caution.

## Ability to Judge Value

Let us continue to pursue the loose analogy between, on one hand, knowing the value of a set of experiences, a social setting, or a portion of a life, and on the other hand Bloggs' knowing that Blech shot Smurf. Conditions have been suggested that would be analogous to Bloggs having been ten feet away from Blech and Smurf and having had a clear view. What might be analogous to Bloggs having good eyesight?

That is not an easy question, and maybe is not one that allows a general answer. Most people know someone whose judgments of value they would generally trust. Sometimes this trust grows out of a set of cases in which they themselves felt confident of a judgment of value, and their judgment was closely matched by that of the person they trust. This may reflect no more than shared taste. But sometimes it is possible to think of it as shared good taste. Also, insofar as the experience of anything that is judged is shaped by the person experiencing it, a background of shared judgments of value makes it seem likely that the one who is trusted will have shaped much the same experience as the one who trusts would have.

Beyond this, some people just seem to us to be unusually sensitive, judicious, and experienced. Perhaps this is the counterpart to Bloggs' good eyesight? Someone who is very sensitive, judicious, and experienced is not thereby an infallible judge of value. Probably there are no infallible judges. But such a person's chances of arriving at an evaluation with which we would largely agree—if we had the experience of what is judged, and also the useful background of relevant experience and practice in sensitivity—will be better than those of the average person.

Ideally a judge of value will have a curious and open mind. This will enable her or him to entertain the possibility that something could have great value even though it is quite different from everything previously experienced that seemed to have great value. Anyone who has struggled with music or poetry in a really new style might assume that the difficulties of appreciating something quite different in life might be like those of coming to terms with drastically innovative works of art. In both cases it cannot be easy, and might require both patience and continued exposure.

What is required to be a reliable judge of value includes experience of things comparable to what is judged. David Hume makes the point, in his essay "On the Standard of Taste," that it would be impossible (however sensitive and intelligent you are) to be a good judge of poetry unless you know some great poetry. Otherwise, a poem that was only slightly better than mediocre might seem—in comparison to everything else one had read—to be really marvelous. Judgments of value are always implicitly comparative. Therefore wide experience of life's possibilities has to be an important qualification for knowledge, or at least a fairly sound opinion, of what has much or little value.

This may seem a disappointingly qualified account of what could make someone a good judge of value. It is true that we can say, in general terms, what would *usually* give someone good qualifications as a judge. But there can be exceptions, in both possible directions. That is, it is always possible that a careful review could make it seem likely that someone who had considerable experience by normal standards was nevertheless not a good judge of value. This might be a counterpart, in relation to value, of having a "tin ear" for music. Conversely, someone of limited experience might turn out, on a careful and reasonable review, to be unusually sensitive to values and thereby a reliable judge.

A further disappointment, on my account, is the variety of cases in which we would very much like to make a judgment of value, but really have little (or maybe nothing) to go on. Are there judgments of value that we are not really well equipped to make? It seems to me that there are two such classes. One consists of judgments of the value of experiences or social settings that are embedded in forms of life that are significantly alien to us, and significantly alien to anyone whose judgments we normally would trust. We may well have our first reactions and our opinions, but these will fall well short of what is required for knowledge. To live like "those people" may seem repugnant, and of little value; perhaps patient investigation would provide considerable grounds for confidence that we were right. But, absent a strong sense of what it is like to live like "those people" (or testimony from reliable judges who have such a sense), our judgments will remain at the level of opinion.

Here is a second class of judgments of value that (to my regret) we seem not well equipped to make. These judgments concern the intrinsic value—that is, the value apart from causal contributions to various good experiences—of the nonsentient portions of nature. By "nonsentient" I mean the parts of nature that do not have minds, experiences, or mental processes.

One way of seeing the problem is as follows. Dogs and cats, like us, are sentient; they have experiences and mental processes. We might well think that the life of a dog or a cat has some value, even apart from any enjoyment that the dog or cat provides to humans. It is possible to have a vague idea of the dog's or cat's experiences and mental processes, and to think that to exist like this is, in itself, worth more than zero. Contrast this with a beautiful world. It can provide wonderful experiences to us if we get to see it. But suppose that nobody does. Is the existence of the beautiful world, in itself, valuable, in much the way as is our existence or that of dogs and cats?

Many environmentalists would like to claim that nonsentient portions of nature have considerable intrinsic value, above and beyond the fact that they cause our valuable experiences of them. It is not clear how this could be established or, on the other hand, how it could be refuted.

It is important to say that such a claim is not required by environmentalist views. A strong environmentalist position can be defended on the basis of goodness as a means. Various elements in nature, such as forests, mountains, and canyons are reliable means to valuable experiences of them by sentient beings, including of course people in future generations.

These environmental elements deserve protection, in this view, because of the valuable experiences they make possible.

Do they have value also in themselves? Would a beautiful world, one devoid of sentient life and that never will be experienced by sentient beings, yet have value? The early twentieth century philosopher G. E. Moore, relying on what he called "intuition," gave an answer of "Yes."[6] I would like to say "Yes" also. But the account thus far given of what places us in a position to judge value leads inexorably to the conclusion that we cannot know.

## Can There Be Knowledge of Value?

The conclusion thus far is that, even in areas in which there can be knowledge of value, we by and large do not know much. Most of us will have some opinions that will have some reasonable basis of support, and that arguably are likely to be correct. But to speak of "knowledge" implies a high standard. Often, grounds for uncertainty as to whether we know enough about, or adequately appreciate, what we are judging limit the degree of reasonable confidence we should have. Room for doubt as to whether our sensitivity or level of experience is fully adequate also should limit our degree of confidence, in many cases.

This result is a modest skepticism, which has some advantages. It can be conducive to keeping an open mind, and attempting to learn more about what we are judging. Should we go further, and accept a complete skepticism of claims to knowledge of values? Many philosophers have suggested that we should, and this represents a live issue in the technical literature of philosophy.

My view is that complete skepticism would be unwarranted. This can be explained by examining possible grounds for complete skepticism, and showing why nothing in these grounds does justify complete skepticism.

Here are four reasons why some philosophers would challenge any claim to knowledge of value:

(1) There cannot be knowledge if there is nothing for the knowledge to be about. Are there value facts? If not, then so-called knowledge of value would really be knowledge of nothing.

6. G. E. Moore, *Principia Ethica* (Cambridge: Cambridge University Press, 1903), 83–4.

(2) Much of what we consider knowledge involves consensus among qualified judges. This is largely true of scientific knowledge. But people keep
disagreeing about what has value. Perhaps then there are no right
answers?

(3) To know something not only requires a right answer; it also requires
that the right answer is one that you wouldn't accept unless it was right.
If someone has a belief about value, is there a causal connection
between the correctness of the belief and the fact that the person
believes it? Or is what people believe about value just a result of
upbringing and general cultural influences?

(4) Knowledge is supposed to be rational. But what people believe about
value appears to have a great deal to do with their emotions. So, what is
there to distinguish, say, "Close affectionate personal relations can have
considerable value" from "Hurray for close affectionate personal relations"?

The reply to (1) has to start from examining hidden assumptions in the
objection. It is easy to imagine facts as being like bulky objects, "furniture
of the universe." But the entities studied by physics are objects and forces;
facts emerge in the intelligent examination of this subject matter. Some
philosophers have argued, because of this, that facts contain what amount
to interpretative structures and are not simply items in the universe.[7]
Physics is about objects and forces; similarly, judgments of value are about
experiences, social settings, portions of lives, etc.

"Is a fact that" is, in ordinary speech, interchangeable with "is the case
that." It has been argued accordingly that there are ethical facts. An example provided by Elizabeth Anscombe is that, after she had ordered potatoes from her grocer, she owed him the money for the potatoes (which
implies that she had an obligation to pay him).[8] If it is the case that, in
most people's experience, close affectionate personal relations can have
considerable value, why can we not say that it is a fact that close affectionate personal relations can have considerable value?

The reply to (2) has to grant some of what the objection claims. At
the frontiers of the sciences there often is little consensus, but it is true
that there is a general tendency for consensus to grow over time.
Conversely, some judgments of value are very widely shared (e.g., that

---

7. See P. F. Strawson, "Truth," *Supplementary Proceedings of the Aristotelian Society* 24
(1950), 129–56; also Bede Rundle, *Facts* (London: Duckworth, 1992).

8. G. E. M. Anscombe, "Modern Moral Philosophy, *Philosophy* 33 (1958), 1–10

extreme pain over a considerable period of time has considerable negative value), but this degree of consensus about value is the exception
rather than the rule.

This is linked to the ways in which judgments of value characteristical-
ly are central to the person we are or would like to become. Given the great
differences among persons, we may find the usual lack of consensus about
value not surprising. Even though personalities occasionally do enter into
the sciences, overall there is a tendency to expect impersonal judgment.

What should we make of this broad contrast? At one extreme, we
could discount it entirely and insist that there are two areas of knowledge
(scientific knowledge and knowledge of value) that admittedly have different features; but that both involve correct judgments that can amount
to knowledge, and that confidence levels in these judgments can and
should be comparable. At the other extreme, we could hold that the fact
that it is very often unreasonable to expect consensus in judgments of
value destroys any claim that judgments of value can be correct, or that
there can be knowledge of value. An intermediate response is to hold onto
the view that we are talking about two areas of knowledge, in which
judgments can be correct and well based, but to concede that confidence
levels very often should be lower in one than in the other. Perhaps there
is even more of a premium on keeping an open mind in judgments of
value than there is in the sciences?

This intermediate response is the one that seems most reasonable. The
first-mentioned response ignores the ways in which a pattern of shared
responses (in which we can gain confidence in our judgments because
others see things in much that way) works as a fail-safe mechanism in relation to personal fallibility. If trained observers generally reach the same
judgments that we do, this surely justifies greater confidence.

The response at the opposite extreme would seem to place all putative
forms of knowledge on a procrustean bed.[9] What logic connects the claim
that very often we cannot expect consensus in judgments of value with
the conclusion that such judgments cannot be correct? There surely is no

---

9. Those not familiar with the story of Procrustes should know that he seized travelers
and placed them on a bed. If they were shorter than the bed, he painfully stretched
their bodies until they fit; if they were taller, he cut off parts of their bodies until they
fit. Plainly he was against diversity in human height. His philosophical counterparts are
those who argue for specious generalizations that they claim to fit an entire range of
cases, with no attention paid to diversity among the cases.

logical contradiction in the notion of correct propositions about which, nevertheless, people cannot entirely agree.

Further, there *are* some ethical propositions on which virtually everyone would agree. These include Anscombe's claim that, her grocer having delivered the potatoes she ordered, she ought to pay. In the realm of value it would include the judgment that it is horrible—has great negative value—to be tortured for weeks at a time. If consensus is what matters, then there should be no objection to holding that these ethical propositions are known. But then, can we rule out the possibility that judgments of value which now are controversial might at some future date attract consensus? And why can't some people know that they are correct before everyone does?

Let us look then more closely at the intermediate response. It seems plausible to insist, on one hand, that people can get something right even if not everyone agrees and, on the other, that lack of consensus can weaken (but not necessarily destroy) any sense that confidence in a judgment is warranted. One implication of this is that knowledge (which typically requires a high level of justified confidence in the right answer) will be harder to get with a lack of consensus. Arguably though there are contentious judgments of value that meet a reasonable standard for knowledge. The best candidates are founded on experience of what is judged and also experiences of a variety of other things that would be compared to it, and are judgments that would be widely (although not universally) shared by others who generally would be considered to be perceptive, judicious, and mature. Why should we not say that the people making these judgments are in a position to be confident of them, and why should we not contrast these as cases of "knowledge" with cases (representing mere opinion) of offhand judgments made by inexperienced people?

Objection (3) involves an oversimplification of something genuine. It is true that upbringing and general cultural influences have a great influence on the judgments of value that people make. In some cases they may be the whole story. But to slide from this to the assumption that in every case they are the entire story appears entirely unwarranted.

Sometimes we are surprised by how wonderful, or how dreary, something is. People who are caught within a pattern of life sometimes are forced to confront the fact that it seems peculiarly unsatisfying to them, even though they had been told that it would have much value. Sometimes, because of such confrontations, people actually go against value judgments of their parents, their teachers, and their cultures.

In some of these cases, all of the same, our considered opinion might be that the breakaway judgment was a mistake. Also it has to be granted that the person who confronts and rejects value judgments of her or his parents, teachers, and culture is more than likely to have a personal history which led to this apparent liberation. This is undoubtedly true, however, also in relation to scientific discoveries or apparent discoveries.

The point is that (1) there are cases in which it looks very plausible that someone has come to realize something about what has value, and (2) even if personal history (including factors that encourage independent thinking) plays a role in this, there will be another factor. The person who claims to have realized something about value can say, "The reason that I came to judge that such-and-such was wonderful (or dreary) was that it *was* wonderful (or dreary)."

The claim is that the value feature—that there really is this value—plays a causal role in relation to the judgment made of value. This corresponds to experiences that very many people sometimes have, of seeming to encounter for themselves how valuable or awful various things are. Should we reject such claims out of hand?[10]

Here is a reply to objection (4). It has been suggested in this book (especially in the discussion of Myth 4) that emotions play a crucial role in judgments of value. Emotions, however, should not be thought of as sheer feeling. Typically they include a central component of judgment as well as elements of feeling and motivation. What we fear, for example, is typically judged to be dangerous; this, as much as any adrenalin rush and desire to get away, makes fear what it is.

There are no obvious reasons why such judgments cannot be correct. Perhaps they begin as implicit elements in a complex that includes inchoate feeling. We feel distaste, and only after a while arrive at the articulated thought, "That is an awful thing." All the same, it may be that what

---

10. There are tangled issues here concerning causation. Can we have some kind of direct awareness of what caused us to have a thought or a feeling, or to arrive at a judgment? (Such direct awareness would not preclude the possibility of error. We can know in many cases what goes on in our thinking, even if sometimes we get it wrong.) Elizabeth Anscombe (*Intention* [Ithaca: Cornell University Press, 1969], 16) gives the following example of what looks like direct awareness of causation: you can know that your fright was caused by the hideous face that appeared at the window. It seems equally possible that you know that your firm conviction that it is awful to be tortured for weeks is caused by your having witnessed or experienced it.

emotionally comes to seem something awful really *is* awful. What delights us or what we admire often is indeed delightful or admirable, and our judgment that this is the case will be at the core of our delight or admiration. There is no clear reason to think that emotional states like delight, admiration, disgust, or boredom cannot be revelatory of what is the case.

This completes the defensive portion of the argument that there can be knowledge of value. The positive portion is simply as follows. People often have a sense of having experienced how much value, or lack of value, various things have. In some of these cases, it looks reasonable to suppose that they have got it pretty much right; that what they value really does have value, or that what they disvalue really is boring, empty, or abhorrent. In the absence of a compelling argument on the other side, it is plausible to suppose that, in these cases, people are aware of how much value something has. This awareness reasonably can be termed knowledge, when someone who has it is confident of her or his judgment and appears generally reliable as a judge of value.[11]

11. The reader may consider this chapter an introduction to a difficult topic, one that has not been adequately explored by philosophers. A more complicated account is found in my "The Epistemology of Non-Instrumental Value," *Philosophy and Phenomenological Research* (2005), which in particular considers disparities between immediate and retrospective judgments of value.

# Bibliography

Alloy, L. B., and Abramson, L. Y. (1979) "Judgment of Contingency in Depressed and Nondepressed Subjects. Sadder But Wiser?" *Journal of Experimental Psychology: General* 108, 441–85.

Ames, Roger T. (1999) "The Chinese Conception of Selfhood," *A Companion to World Philosophies,* eds. Eliot Deutsch and Ron Bontekoe (Oxford: Blackwell Publishers), 148–54.

Anscombe, G.E.M. (1958) "Modern Moral Philosophy," *Philosophy* 33, 1–10.

——— (1969) *Intention* (Ithaca: Cornell University Press).

Argyle, Michael (1987) *The Psychology of Happiness* (London: Methuen).

——— (2000) *Psychology and Religion. An Introduction* (London: Routledge).

Aristotle (4th c. BCE/1999) *The Nicomachean Ethics,* trans. Terence Irwin, Second Edition (Indianapolis: Hackett Publishing Co.).

Armon-Jones, Claire (1991) *Varieties of Affect* (Hemel Hempstead: Harvester Wheatsheaf; Toronto: University of Toronto Press).

Block, Gay, and M. Drucker (1992) *Rescuers: Portraits of Moral Courage in the Holocaust* (New York: Holmes and Meier).

Brecht, Bertolt (1998) "Socrates Wounded," *Collected Stories,* eds. John Willett and Ralph Manheim (New York: Arcade/Little, Brown), 139–53.

Brickman, P., D. Coates, and R. Janoff-Bulman (1978) "Lottery Winners and Accident Victims: Is Happiness Relative?" *Journal of Personality and Social Psychology* 37, 917–27.

Calhoun, C., and R. Solomon (eds.) (1984) *What Is an Emotion?* (New York: Oxford University Press).

Camus, Albert (1955) *The Myth of Sisyphus,* trans. Justin O'Brien (New York: Vintage Books).

Chuang-Tzu (4th c. BCE/2001) *Chuang-Tzu the Inner Chapters,* trans. A. C. Graham (Indianapolis: Hackett Publishing Co.).

Confucius (5th c. BCE/2003) *The Analects,* trans. Edward Slingerland (Indianapolis: Hackett Publishing Co.).

——— (5th c. BCE/1938) trans. Arthur Waley (New York: Vintage Books).

Csikszentmihalyi, Mihaly (1990) *Flow: The Psychology of Optimal Experience* (New York: Harper & Row).

*Daodejing (Tao Te Ching)* (2002), trans. Philip J. Ivanhoe (Indianapolis: Hackett Publishing Co.).

——— (2001), trans. R. B. Blakney as *The Way of Life* (New York: Signet Books).

David-Neel, Alexandra (1929/1971) *Magic and Mystery in Tibet* (New York: Dover).

Diener, Ed, and R. E. Lucas (1999) "Personality and Subjective Well-Being," *Well-Being: The Foundations of Hedonic Psychology,* eds. D. Kahneman, E. Diener, and N. Schwartz (New York: Russell Sage Foundation), 213–29.

Frederick and Loewenstein (1999) "Hedonic Adaptation," Kahneman et al., eds., *Well-Being,* 302–329.

Frederickson (2000) "Extracting Meaning from Past Affective Experiences: The Importance of Peaks, Ends, and Specific Emotions," *Cognition and Emotion* 14, 577–606.

Fridja, Nico (1993) "Moods, Emotion Episodes, and Emotions," *Handbook of Emotions,* eds. M. Lewis and J. M. Haviland (New York: Guilford Press), 381–403.

Funder, David (1999) *Personality Judgment: A Realistic Approach to Person Perception* (San Diego: Academic Press).

Hartshorne, Hugh, M. A. May, and F. K. Shuttleworth (1930) *Studies in the Organization of Character* (New York: Macmillan).

Herodotus (5th c. BCE/1934) *The History of Herodotus,* trans. George Rawlinson (New York: Tudor Publishing Company).

Hume, David (1742/1985) "The Sceptic," *Essays,* ed. Eugene Miller (Indianapolis: Liberty Fund), 159–80.

—— (1751/1983) *An Enquiry Concerning the Principles of Morals,* ed. J.B. Schneewind (Indianapolis: Hackett Publishing Co.).

Kahneman, Daniel (1999) "Objective Happiness," Kahneman et al., eds., *Well-Being* (New York: Russell Sage), 3–25.

—— (2000) "Experienced Utility and Objective Happiness. A Moment-Based Approach," *Choices, Values, and Frames,* eds. D. Kahneman and A. Tversky (Cambridge: Cambridge University Press), 673–9.

Kant, Immanuel (1785/1981) *Grounding of the Metaphysics of Morals,* trans. James Ellington (Indianapolis: Hackett Publishing Co.).

Kierkegaard, Soren (1969) *Fear and Trembling* and *The Sickness Unto Death,* trans. Walter Lowrie (Princeton: Princeton University Press).

—— (1941) *Concluding Unscientific Postscript,* trans. David F. Swenson and Walter Lowrie (Princeton: Princeton University Press).

Kupperman, Joel J. (1984–5) "Character and Self-Knowledge," *Proceedings of the Aristotelian Society* 85, 219–38.

—— (1995) "An Anti-Essentialist View of the Emotions," *Philosophical Psychology* 8, 341–51.

—— (2001) *Classic Asian Philosophy: A Guide to the Essential Texts* (New York: Oxford University Press).

—— (2005a) "Morality, Ethics, and Wisdom," in *Handbook of Wisdom: Psychological Perspectives,* eds. Robert Sternberg and Jennifer Jordan (Cambridge: Cambridge University Press), 245–71.

—— (2005b) "A New Look at the Logic of the 'Is'–'Ought' Relation," *Philosophy* 80, 345–61.

—— (2005c) "The Epistemology of Non-Instrumental Value," *Philosophy and Phenomenological Research.*

Langer, Ellen (1989) *Mindfulness* (Reading, Mass.: Addison Wesley).

La Rochefoucauld, Francois, duc de (1695/1959) *Maxims,* trans. L.W. Tancock (Baltimore: Penguin Books).

Macintyre, Alasdair (1978) *After Virtue* (Notre Dame: University of Notre Dame Press).

Malcolm, Norman (1958) *Ludwig Wittgenstein. A Memoir.* (London: Oxford University Press).

Mencius (4th c. BCE/1970) *Mencius,* trans. D. C. Lau (Harmondsworth: Penguin).

Mill, John Stuart (1859/1978) *On Liberty,* ed. Elizabeth Rappaport (Indianapolis: Hackett Publishing Co.).

—— (1861/1979) *Utilitarianism,* ed. George Sher (Indianapolis: Hackett Publishing Co.).

Moore, G. E. (1903) *Principia Ethica* (Cambridge: Cambridge University Press).

Morris, Ivan I. (1975) *The Nobility of Failure: Tragic Heroes in the History of Japan* (New York: Holt, Rinehart, and Winston).

Newman, Ira (1984) "Fiction and Discovery," Ph.D. diss., University of Connecticut.

Nietzsche, Friedrich (1886/1989) *Beyond Good and Evil,* trans. Walter Kaufmann (New York: Vintage Books).

Paton, H. J. (1953–4) "An Alleged Right to Lie: A Problem in Kantian Ethics," *Kant Studien* 45, 190–203.

Plato (4th c. BCE/1937) *Apology,* in *The Dialogues of Plato,* trans. B. Jowett, vol. 1 (New York: Random House).

—— (4th c. BCE/1993) *Philebus,* trans. Dorothea Frede (Indianapolis: Hackett Publishing Co.).

—— (4th c. BCE/1992) *Republic,* trans. G. M. A. Grube, rev. C. D. C. Reeve.

*The Questions of King Milinda* (1963) trans. T. W. Rhys Davids (New York: Dover Books).

Reps, P., and N. Senzaki, eds. (1985) *Zen Flesh, Zen Bones.* (Boston: Tuttle).

Rozin, Paul, Jonathan Haidt, and Clark McCauley (1993) "Disgust," *Handbook of the Emotions,* eds. M. Lewis and J. M. Haviland (New York: Guilford Press), 575–94.

Rozin, Paul, and Ed Royzman (1999) "Negativity Bias, Negativity Dominance, and Contagion," *Personality and Social Psychology Review* 5, 296–320.

Rundle, Bede (1992) *Facts* (London: Duckworth).

Sartre, Jean-Paul (1956) *Being and Nothingness,* trans. Hazel Barnes (New York: Philosophical Library).

Seligman, Martin (2002) *Authentic Happiness* (New York: Simon and Schuster).

Sennett, Richard, and Jonathan Cobb (1972) *The Hidden Injuries of Class* (New York: Knopf).

Smith, Michael (2003) "Neutral and Relative Value After Moore," *Ethics* 113, 576–98.

Solomon, Robert C. (1976) *The Passions* (Garden City, NY: Anchor/Doubleday).

Strawson, P. F. (1950) "Truth," *Supplementary Proceedings of the Aristotelian Society* 24, 129–56.

*Tao Te Ching* (see *Daodejing*).

Twain, Mark (1985) "The Man That Corrupted Hadleyburg," in *Mark Twain's Short Stories,* ed. Justin Kaplan (New York: Signet Books).

Unamuno, Miguel de (1962) *The Tragic Sense of Life,* trans. J. E. C. Flitch (London: Fontana).

Vasari, Giorgio (1998) *The Lives of the Artists,* trans. Julia Conaway Bondonella and Peter Bondonella (Oxford: Oxford World Classics).

Wittgenstein, Ludwig (1953) *Philosophical Investigations,* trans. G. E. M. Anscombe (London: Macmillan Books).

Zhuangzi (see Chuang Tzu).

# APPENDIX

Note: These entries are intended to provide fuller (although hardly exhaustive) treatment of deeper or more complicated issues relevant to the text, especially in the opening chapter.

1. Here are two reasons why many are suspicious of the view that people can be wrong about what they think are values in their lives. One is that most of us prefer to live in a highly tolerant society, and such judgments risk undermining attitudes of tolerance. The fear is that such judgments, especially if they are voiced, can lead to unacceptable pressure on people who are "different."

A second reason is that it is plausible to suppose that there are many kinds of very good lives. Some great philosophers (for example Aristotle) have talked as if there is only one kind. If one comes to think that this is a mistake, then a natural thought is that someone whose quality of life looks rather low may have a different set of highly positive values from what one is used to. It is often extremely hard to grasp the texture and intricacy of another person's life. Because of this, we can be blind to genuine values that are unfamiliar. This reflection can lead to a general skepticism about judgments of lives other than one's own, and a refusal to make such judgments.

These reasons have some weight. Are they compelling? It can be argued on the other side that judgments of the quality of life of other people can normally be both tentative and tacit, and also can be combined with a high degree of tolerance of differences. John Stuart Mill, whose *On Liberty* made a strong case for liberal tolerance, thought all the same that we could very well judge that another person was foolish or tasteless. (See *On Liberty,* ed. Elizabeth Rapaport [Indianapolis: Hackett Publishing Co., 1978], p. 77.)

Also, while judging others' lives (even tacitly) has its risks, refusing to make such judgments is likely to have great costs. Absent such judgments, how can one have any reflective sense of the best direction of one's own life? Often we get ideas about our own basic choices from noting how some people seem to know how to live, and how others have lives that in all probability no one should want.

Whatever are the pragmatic considerations, it seems clear that judgments of the quality of life can be meaningfully made from the outside. We can understand what they mean. We typically have some sense of what would count in their favor or against them.

Whether they always can be well-founded is a further question. It is highly arguable that often the intelligent choice is to suspend judgment, because one

149

does not know or understand enough to judge. "It might be a very rich life, in ways I cannot grasp" can be a reasonable thought. There is a large area between real doubt and entire assurance, within which we could say to ourselves such things as: "Unless I am missing something, that looks like an extremely constricted and unrewarding life" or "It looks like an extremely rewarding life, but perhaps there are tensions or psychic costs that one does not see at first." There usually are reasons for caution in making judgments of values in a life not one's own, but refusal to have even a provisional opinion goes beyond ordinary caution.

2. Let me anticipate an objection to my suggestion that Csikszentmihalyi's data show that some pleasures are worth more than others. It may be said that, if people value most the pleasures of being caught up in the flow of skilled activity, then surely these pleasures are greater or more intense. This would preserve the simple view that pleasure is pleasure, and that all that matters is strength or intensity of pleasure.

This view is too simple because of the mixture of elements in pleasure. These include felt affect, and also the degree of preference that the pleasurable experience continue or be repeated. Further, there may be variation between the degree of preference at the time and at later moments. Someone who concentrates on degree of preference at the time might conclude that eating potato chips (which notoriously is hard to stop) is far more pleasant than drinking fine wine. The fine wine might score better in affect, and also in degree of preference at some later moment to repeat the experience. There are multiple sources, rather than a single source, of answers to questions of how strong a pleasure is or was. Certainly, felt affect has especially great weight.

In the case of skilled activities, this crucial factor of strength of affect at the time usually would not parallel the high value usually given to the pleasures of flow. This is particularly true because of the mixture of effort with satisfaction that such pleasures often involve. They rank higher in their scoring by people who experience them than they do in felt affect. Hence the value typically assigned to such pleasures is out of proportion to what their strength or intensity (by normal standards) is.

3. My suggestion that psychological data support some conclusions about values takes sides in a long-running philosophical debate. This concerns the relation between the "is" and the "ought," or facts and values (in the broad sense of "values" that includes matters of how we should behave, as well as what is rewarding in life). Many philosophers have claimed that the "ought" cannot be logically derived from the "is," or that there is no logical relation between the two. The eighteenth century Scottish philosopher David Hume at one point makes the first claim. The early twentieth century philosopher G. E. Moore has been held to make the second claim, and at various points more recently R. M. Hare made it also.

The first of these claims (the one that denies logical derivability) is less strong, and therefore perhaps more plausible than the first. It does look plausible to say that descriptive statements about what the world is like do not entail ethical judgments. That is, it is plausible to hold that, even if we know all we need to know about what the world is like, what would be best or would be obligatory remains (logically) an open question. If this is accepted, then someone who agrees with a set of descriptive statements is never logically compelled to accept any particular set of ethical conclusions.

But the descriptive statements arguably might provide genuine reasons (less strong than entailment) for ethical conclusions, such that even someone who rejected the conclusions might be able to say "Yes, these are good reasons, and they strengthen the case; but still I do not accept the conclusions." Moore nowhere appears to have room for the idea that descriptive reasons can provide a kind of logical support to ethical conclusions. (His view is that judgments of what is good are provided by "intuition.") Hare explicitly rejects the idea that there can be logical support weaker than entailment.

In short, there are at least three main positions on this issue: (1) descriptive statements can entail ethical statements; (2) descriptive statements can provide logical support, short of entailment, for ethical conclusions; (3) there can be no logical relation between descriptive statements and ethical conclusions. What is at issue is enormously complicated. Relevant questions include "What counts as a purely descriptive statement?," "What are facts?," and also, "Are there more kinds of logical reasoning than merely deductive (reasoning about entailments) and inductive (reasoning about the probability of known patterns repeating themselves)?"

None of these questions is simple. The one about facts is especially thorny. Philosophers who talk about facts and values rarely go to the trouble of explaining what a fact is, and at least one influential philosopher (P. F. Strawson) has argued that facts involve interpretative constructions and hence "are not in the world." (See P. F. Strawson, "Truth," *Supplementary Proceedings of the Aristotelian Society* 24 [1950], 129–56; also Bede Rundle, *Facts* [London: Duckworth, 1992].) Elizabeth Anscombe claimed that it was a "brute fact" (although clearly it also was an ethical judgment about obligations) that she owed money to her grocer for potatoes that he had delivered. (See G. E. M. Anscombe, "Modern Moral Philosophy," *Philosophy* 33 [1958], 1–10.)

The position on this issue that underlies my use of psychological data is the middle one. (See my "A New Look at the Logic of the 'Is'–'Ought' Relation," *Philosophy* 80 [2005], 345–61.) Psychological data do not provide conclusive reasons for ethical conclusions in my view: there is no entailment. But sometimes they do provide good reasons, because of connections of meaning between ethical claims and some kinds of descriptive statements.

4. Here is a case for holding that Mill was right in claiming a deep connection between desire and pleasure. It can be argued that the difference between, on one hand, desiring something and, on the other hand, merely preferring it in a cool reflective way, is the pleasure (or escape from pain) associated with the cases that involve desire. The pleasure or escape from pain could be part of what is expected

if one gets what one desires. Sometimes though people desire outcomes that they know will not be pleasant (e.g., martyrdom in what they think is a good cause), when the thought of the outcome is pleasant to them even if the reality will not be. There also are instances of obsessive desire, in which not doing something is thought of as painful. The point is that the word "desire" traditionally has a meaning that separates it from merely having a preference. In any of these kinds of case, there would not be "desire" if pleasure or escape from pain were not involved.

If Mill is right about the desire-pleasure connection, this seems actually to weaken his claim that desire is *the* sense of value. Why can't we give special weight to judgments of value that result from cool reflective preference that lacks the warmth and urgency of desire?

5. Emotions typically have three elements. There is room for philosophical debate as to which is most important, and also whether any or all of them count as essential. Traditionally the element of feeling, the experienced affect of an emotion, drew the most attention. In the last few decades, many philosophers and psychologists have played down the element of feeling, regarding it as inessential, and have placed judgment (viewed as putatively cognitive) at the core of emotion. The major philosophical pioneer in this has been Robert Solomon (see his *The Passions* [Garden City, NY: Doubleday Anchor, 1966]). Fear in this view is first and foremost the judgment that something (the object of the fear) is dangerous; anger is the judgment that someone has done something untoward and not readily forgivable. One modification of this has been suggested by Claire Armon-Jones (see her *Varieties of Affect* [Hemel Hempstead: Harvester Wheatsheaf; Toronto: University of Toronto Press, 1991]). In some cases one does not judge that the feared object is dangerous. Rather one construes it as (sees it as) dangerous. Someone who is a phobic of snakes, for example, can know perfectly well that the garter snake is not dangerous but nevertheless see it as frightening.

The third typical element is motivational. Normally we expect someone who experiences fear to be motivated either to flee or to oppose whatever is the object of the fear. (This motivation may be overcome by contrary pulls, such as the desire to look nonchalant; but all the same it is present, and under suitable circumstances can manifest itself.) In the case of pleasure, the normal motivation is to have more. This too can be overriden, say, by a desire not to be self-indulgent. But if, even in the absence of any overriding contrary motivation, someone declines opportunities to repeat an experience, we have reason to doubt that it was pleasant. The reason need not be absolutely compelling. There can be cases in which something was only slightly pleasant, and the person who experienced it prefers a variety of pleasures rather than repetition of the same one.

An attractively simple view is that any case of emotion involves all three elements. But there are problems with this. Someone may have what we consider an emotion (say anger, or love), but because of preoccupation with a set of actions or a kind of denial (of the emotion) does not have the feeling normally associated with the emotion. Arguably it is not always the case that someone who is angry *feels* angry, or that someone who is in love *feels* love. Sometimes the feeling is delayed even while other aspects of the emotion can be evident to a trained observer. Can judgment or construal of an object be absent from an emotion? Think of emotions that people find in music. (Is the sadness you experience while listening to sad music sadness about something?) It is also hard to rule out possible cases in which people have feelings, make the judgments that go along with those feelings, but seem devoid of the corresponding motivations. So perhaps all we can say is that each of the three elements is typically found in emotions, and beyond this that we would be highly unlikely to term something an emotion that did not include at least one or two of them.

6. It is important to distinguish suffering from pain. Familiar examples of pain without suffering are people caught up in activities that require concentration, say in wartime or during a rescue operation, who have been hurt but are not bothered by the pain until after their activities are completed. The training given to women preparing for childbirth does not eliminate the possibility of pain, but is designed to eliminate suffering by introducing an element of personal control, thus focusing attention away from the pain. Finally, a nice anecdote about pain and suffering appears in an early twentieth century travel book, written by Alexandra David-Neel, who moved through Tibet disguised as a man. She reports an incident in which a Buddhist monk, traveling with temple treasure, was stabbed by the acolyte traveling with him (who made off with the money). The dying man asked the police to cut short their questioning, because (he said) he preferred not to suffer, and therefore wished to enter a meditative state in which the suffering would not be present. (See David-Neel, *Magic and Mystery in Tibet* [New York: Dover Books, 1971], 16.)

Pains of various sorts can occur to almost anyone, and pains of the sort that involve stimulation of pain receptors in the body can occur even to a Buddhist adept. Suffering involves being captured by the pain. The etymology suggests an essential element of passivity in suffering. (It is no accident that both women trained in childbirth techniques and the Buddhist monk in David-Neel's story avoid suffering by taking control of their experiences.)

Further, we normally would not speak of suffering that predictably lasts (and that the sufferer knows will last) only an extremely short period of time. However intense the negative experience, that would be agony, not suffering. Suffering typically is a state of mind that not only feels negative and carries with it a sense of lack of control, but also involves a sense of there being no end in sight (even though in fact death can cut short someone's suffering after a brief period).

7. Daniel Kahneman has suggested that what Brickman et al. had demonstrated is not really a hedonic (pleasure) treadmill, but rather a satisfaction treadmill. (See his "Experienced Utility and Objective Happiness. A Moment-Based Approach," in *Choices, Values, and Frames,* eds. D. Kahneman and A. Tversky [Cambridge: Cambridge University Press, 2000], 685 ff.) The thought is that there might be

typically more pleasure than before in the lives of lottery winners, and typically less in the lives of those made paraplegic early in their lives, but that the former now expect more (and the latter less) out of life, so that for both groups the levels of satisfaction remain about the same.

This has a certain intuitive appeal. It connects with the ironic remark of the French singer Maurice Chevalier, who when asked how it was to have reached the age of seventy, replied that it was pretty good considering the alternative. How we feel about bits of our lives will depend on what is treated as a baseline or a standard.

The issue may be more complicated than it looks, though, both philosophically and empirically. Philosophically we need to focus on what pleasure is and what counts as "satisfaction." As we have seen, there are two elements of (and criteria for) pleasure. One is felt affect. The other is that the person who putatively experienced pleasure would like more of the same, or the same again. The second element helps to tell us whether the experience really was pleasant after all, and the strength of the preference also can indicate how pleasant the experience might have been. Clearly our standards, which inevitably are influenced by what we have come to expect (and what the alternatives available to us are), have a considerable role in this second component of pleasure. Is "satisfaction" merely this second component? Or does it also include elements of felt affect, perhaps a broader set (including the affect associated with objectless, global happiness) than that which is characteristic specifically of pleasure?

Here is an empirical complication. Any nonpsychologist will be reduced to drawing from his or her own experience in assessing Kahneman's suggestion. In my case, an example of shifting standards and expectations is connected with my liking for Asian food. At an early stage, really good Chinese food was hard to find in America, and Vietnamese and Thai food were largely unavailable. The pleasure of finding restaurants of this sort abroad, and of early meals in America at a really good Chinese restaurant, was exciting and exhilarating. By and large this is no longer true; when high quality examples of these cuisines are readily available, it is rare to experience excitement and exhilaration. On the other hand, my sense is that a good Asian meal now is at least a bit more pleasant than a mediocre Asian meal was in the old days.

Pleasures are a mixed lot. The ones people usually look forward to most (and sometimes may treasure retrospectively) involve strong elements of excitement and exhilaration. My personal example suggests to me that the hedonic treadmill more than holds for pleasures of this sort. On the other hand, it also suggests that there are pleasures for which reversion to the previous norm is not complete.

This suggests a further point. Might there be in some cases a redistribution within the bundle of pleasures in a person's life? Might someone whose life has been very successful (in terms of preference satisfaction) have a bundle with a higher percentage of pleasures of the quiet and modest kind (and a lower percentage of pleasures connected with exciting surprises)? If so, there could be a real risk that life would seem bland. Might the opposite be true among some of the people who have been defeated by life? This might be connected with the fact that Calcutta, and not Zurich, has been described as a "City of Joy." (The joy here, I am assuming, is often not the diffuse objectless joy of mystics and poets, but rather joy that has specific objects, in which case it looks like a heightened form of pleasure—that, it should be said, can coexist with considerable pain.) If there is any truth to this hypothesis, then the hedonic treadmill should not lose any ground. The overall level of pleasure should remain about the same in improved circumstances of life, factoring in a lower number of sharp and exciting pleasures and a greater number of more modest ones.

8. Here are two separate but closely related problems about the self. First is the problem of personal identity, of what makes someone the same person as the one whom we may have met earlier. This has attracted considerable attention in Western philosophy, ever since John Locke in the late seventeenth century wondered about the imagined case of someone who woke up in a different body (and what the criteria could be for claiming that this was the same person who had gone to sleep in another body). Locke and his immediate successors assumed that the answer to the question, "Is it the same person?" had to be either "Yes" or "No." A strong body of late twentieth century philosophical literature argues that the factors that determine personal identity are a matter of degree, so that there can be cases in which the answer is neither sharply "Yes" nor sharply "No."

More than two thousand years earlier some Buddhist philosophers argued along similar lines. (See *The Questions of King Milinda,* trans. T. W. Rhys Davids [New York: Dover Books, 1963].) Because of this, the view of reincarnation in the philosophical versions of early Buddhism was more equivocal than has been the tendency in popular Buddhism. The analogy suggested in *The Questions of King Milinda* is with a flame on a lit candle being used to light another candle. "Is the flame on the second candle the same as the flame on the original candle?" is one of those questions that does not seem to admit of a clearcut answer. The suggestion is that "Is X a reincarnation of Y?" would be similar in that respect.

Both in the Western and the Buddhist philosophical literature, the problem of personal identity is put in terms of an individual who may or may not be identical with what is putatively another individual. The problem of sense of self moves in a different direction. It concerns the core of a person's self-image. This would play a part in a good answer to the question "Who (or what) are you?"

One connection between this and the problem of personal identity is a background of facts and habits of thought that are relevant to both. The facts principally concern change. You look different and think differently now than you did ten or twelve years ago, and who knows what it will be like thirty or forty years from now? There can be major changes, even in quite ordinary lives. Then, if we imagine cases of waking up in a different body, or of what might or might not be cases of reincarnation, or of having spent a few hundred years in a paradise or a hell, the changes become potentially huge and really unimaginable. Our habits of mind though demand some kind of stable truth. This is especially pronounced in relation to questions of who or what one is.

One way of trying to incorporate stable truth in sense of self is to claim that some personality characteristics are relatively invariant. Indeed, some people are shy, or bold, or given to flights of fancy, or to anxiety, throughout a lifetime. So the strategy is not entirely implausible. Another way, which seems more thoroughly secure, is to treat personal origin as part of who one is. This will include who one's parents were, perhaps ethnicity, the time and place of one's growing up, etc. Even if one moves to a drastically different place and social setting, and even in the imagined case in which one travels in time, these will remain factors of who one is. Rightly or wrongly, many people would regard them as very important factors. A career that is thought of as long-term, and close personal relations of the sort that do not seem transitory, also can be part of the image of who one is.

All of this said, it has to be admitted that a person's social and cultural context can be much more central to sense of self in some cultures than in others. (See Roger Ames, "The Chinese Conception of Selfhood," *A Companion to World Philosophies*, eds. Eliot Deutsch and Ron Bontekoe [Oxford: Blackwell Publishers, 1999], 148–54.) My suggestion is that the differences here are of degree, and that—even in the most individualistic culture—a person's origins and social networks are likely to play some role in her or his sense of self.

9. Vulnerability and invulnerability has been a large topic in some ancient philosophies. Confucius claimed that the happiness of a truly cultivated person could not be ruined, because the major sources of satisfaction for such a person would be internal and hence not subject to luck. The average person cares most about such things as money and social position, and wants good luck in attaining or retaining these. But such things are much less important (in Confucius' view) to someone who is cultivated, who gains satisfaction especially from virtuous actions and the style of personal interactions. Somewhat similar views can be found in Plato and Aristotle.

All three philosophers in varying degrees hold that the happiness of an entirely cultivated person might be impaired but cannot be ruined. Buddha's philosophy is built around an even stronger claim of invulnerability for someone who is enlightened. The claim is that if you lose your desires (even your altruistic desires), and retain only mild preferences (such as those of compassion), you will never suffer. There is room for argument about all of this, and about whether, after all, everyone has a point or an area of extreme vulnerability.

Separate issues occur in relation to people who are not extremely cultivated or (in Buddhist terms) enlightened. Some readers may wonder how the claim (in the discussion of Myth 2) that many people's happiness can be ruined by dire poverty or severe chronic disease squares with the recent psychological data (reported in the first chapter) of hedonic treadmills and adaptations of subjective well-being.

The answer is that the data show a far greater incidence of adaptation than one would have expected, but it is not unlimited. In cases of people rendered paraplegic, for example, there is a pattern of adaptation if it happens early in life but not if it happens late in life. No one to my knowledge has claimed a pattern of adaptation (although there certainly may be individual cases) of people who had been moderately prosperous and then sank into a continuing state of really dire poverty, or for people whose life came to center on severe chronic disease.

Finally, the topic of vulnerability connects with a peculiar asymmetry in many people's possible experiences of life. It is tempting to think of one's ordinary life as at the zero point on a graph, with unusually good experiences or states of being as having positive values and unusually bad ones having negative values. The asymmetry is as follows. The worst imaginable experiences or states of being are (for many people, particularly those who are reasonably prosperous and moderately healthy) much further below the zero point than the best imaginable experiences or states of being are above it.

In order to get a sense of this, try the following thought experiment. Imagine a choice between two months of life pretty much as it has been, or a month of the best you can imagine and a month of the worst that you can imagine. (The order of the two months can be reversed if you prefer.)

My sense is that the vast majority of readers would prefer the two ordinary months to the wonderful-plus-terrible combination. This suggests that the terrible is viewed as more negative than the wonderful is positive. It may well be that this asymmetry in valuations is more pronounced in residents of highly prosperous countries than it might be in places where life is tenuous and desperate. But it may be also that the asymmetry captures something about values and not merely about how people think about them. Some philosophers have portrayed a good human life as depending more than anything on avoiding highly negative experiences. This is central to the philosophies of Buddha and Epicurus, but also it appears in the discussion in Chapter 2 of John Stuart Mill's *Utilitarianism* of what reasonably could be regarded as a happy life.

10. Mencius advocates a limited worry about the future, as a way of avoiding serious problems later. There are some classic Asian philosophical texts, notably the Indian *Bhagavad Gita* and also the Chinese Daoist *Daodejing* and *Zhuangzi* (*Chuang Tzu*), that normally would be read as advocating a more complete lack of emotional concern for the future. It is abundantly clear in all of them, though, that this is not a recommendation for a mindless or careless relation to what will happen next. The Daoist texts especially emphasize the spiritual importance of watchfulness and alertness. (See my *Classic Asian Philosophy: A Guide to the Essential Texts* [New York: Oxford University Press, 2001].)

Mencius, on most interpretations, would not go as far as the *Bhagavad Gita* or the Daoists in wishing to minimize emotions in relation to the future. But he is hardly at the other extreme. He certainly does not recommend an anxious concern for the future. He suggests that an ongoing small degree of emotional investment is like an inoculation, protecting one against anything that might produce strong negative emotions later on. In any event—if we return from Asian philosophy to the ordinary life of most of us—an important point is that the sequences of skilled behavior will hardly take up all of one's waking moments even in the most fulfilling life. One can lose oneself in skilled behavior, and at other times plan (with Mencius' recommended attitudes of mild worry) for the future.

11. Here is one reason why the analogy between awareness of value and being an eyewitness is certainly not a close analogy. A number of philosophers have argued (to my mind convincingly) that knowing that something is good is essentially personal, as opposed to other kinds of knowledge. It enters into the kind of person one is. As Plato puts it, the knower becomes the known. Kierkegaard makes essentially the same point in *Concluding Unscientific Postscript*. Any item of knowledge can accidentally affect the kind of person one is, but in the case of ethical knowledge it is required that it become part of who one is (if it really is knowledge, rather than mere opinion). If one doesn't have a commitment to behave along the lines of what one allegedly knows (in ethics), then it has not, as it were, come home to one.

Can you believe something in ethics without anything like a commitment? In ordinary cases, we doubt the sincerity of someone's statements about what has value (or is right or wrong) if there is not at least some inclination to behave along corresponding lines. But there are cases that are not ordinary, in which someone who affirms ethical judgments entirely contrary to her or his behavioral tendencies yet could be sincere. A person who is perversely diabolical could enjoy doing something *because* he or she believes it is wrong, and someone who is perversely self-loathing could avoid something because he or she believes that it does have value. (The thought might be, "It is too good for me.") In either sort of case, merely affirming a judgment about value looks like mere opinion unless it is accompanied by a strong inclination to act positively in accordance with the value judgment.

12. Is there anything like a sharp distinction between what simply has value (from a neutral point of view) and what has value for some specific person? For an exploration of this contrast, see Michael Smith, "Neutral and Relative Value After Moore," *Ethics* 113 (2003), 576–98. Clearly there is a sense in which something could be good for you, but not good for your neighbors, or vice versa. But usually what is good for you is good, not merely because of its role in your life apart from causal consequences, but also because of its causal consequences. (The causal consequences might be good for you and bad for the neighbors.) Also there is the complication that you might think that something is very good for you because you like it (or want it) so much; the arguments of the first two chapters suggest that this can be a mistake.

In the last analysis, if something really is good for you, quite apart from its causal consequences, this has to be because it really is good, period. There are two complications related to this, though. We might be tempted to say simply that a truly wonderful set of experiences will be good in the context of anyone's life. But it has to be added that the experiences of X will be different in the context of any one of your neighbors' lives than they are for you. Secondly, something can be evaluated not merely in the context of an individual life, but also in a larger context. We might judge that Al Capone (despite his moral turpitude) had a wonderful set of experiences on his holiday, but also might think that in a larger social context it would have been better if someone more deserving had had experiences of that sort